# GOD'S TRUE LOVE
## A LIFE-CHANGING EXPLORATION
## OF THE HEART OF GOD

## DAVID HARWOOD

GOD'S TRUE LOVE
Copyright 2008 David Harwood
ISBN: 978-1-886296-49-7
Printed in the United States of America
All rights reserved.

Cover Design: Charles Ciepiel
Photograph used by permission of Massimiliano Lattanzi

Arrow Publications, Inc.
P.O. Box 10102
Cedar Rapids, IA 52410
Phone: (319) 395-7388
Fax: (319) 395-7353

# Table of Contents

Acknowledgements

Introduction

## PART 1: RESTORING A BIBLICAL PERSPECTIVE

Chapter 1: Jesus, the Beloved Son    13

Chapter 2: Witnesses from the Inner Circle    23

Chapter 3: Paul's Pattern    39

Chapter 4: Grasping the Love of God    51

Chapter 5: The Promised Outcome    65

## PART 2: *AGAPE*

Chapter 6: A New Perspective    81

Chapter 7: The Array of *Agape*    97

Chapter 8: What is God's Love Like?    109

## PART 3: RESTORING THE GOSPEL

Chapter 9: What is Man?    133

Chapter 10: Why is Man?    147

## PART 4: PURSUING

Chapter 11: Overcoming Obstacles    171

Chapter 12: Pursue Love    191

Bibliography

About the *Love of God* Project

# Acknowledgements

THE KERNEL OF THIS WORK was sown in me through two spiritual encounters during the 80s and illumination and interpretation in the early 90s. I am grateful for the stewardship of this message and want to acknowledge the God of Israel, who never changes.

This book reflects the encouragement, prayer, and work of several people. Paul wrote, "Render to all what is due them…honor to whom honor." (Romans 13:7) In seeking to give honor where honor is due I delight to acknowledge the following:

Special thanks to Mike Snyder and Dr. Michael Brown.

Katie George labored long and hard in editing and organizing this material. My daughter, Shira, invested herself in providing necessary and insightful editorial help.

Kimberly and Marianne (two faithful intercessors from our congregation) read this material when it was scattered notes and essays. Surprisingly, they encountered God through it. This was very encouraging.

Harry and Louise Bizzell have hosted Elaine and me innumerable times over the last thirty years. I appreciate their insight, friendship and hospitality. O. J. Partington would frequently visit and mentor us. He was a wonderful friend. Nick Welch was the older brother I never had. I miss Jim and Nick but thank God for their lasting encouragement.

These friends have especially encouraged and challenged me during this process: Ron, Mike and Rob, B, Barry, Eddie, Carl and Stan.

Thank you Robin and Tom. Lance, Leon and Ron, I appreciate your timely encouragement.

Thank you Lindsey, Cary, Matt and Elita, Lesley, and Rafael for co-laboring with us. Thanks Brad for providing an outlet into Long Island.

There are others who have read, encouraged, and prayed over this book. Some have given advice and financial support. I am grateful.

New Covenant Community of Believers has been graciously supportive in time, involvement, and prayer.

My parents have demonstrated godly principles of marriage throughout my life. They have my abiding respect and affection.

Shira, Jonathan and Benjamin are deeply beloved. I love my kids.

My wife and best friend, Elaine, has been exceptionally supportive. Nobody could ask for a better partner in life or ministry.

# Introduction

ONE SUMMER, IN THE BASEMENT of a church in Manhattan, I had the opportunity to teach a course built upon the contents of this book. That first day was…interesting. I stood facing thirty students. They were like a spiritual Special Forces detachment. It soon became apparent that some of them felt studying the love of God was irrelevant to their ministry goals or too elementary to be worth an investment of their time and effort. I looked at the staff. Some were skeptical. Their experience led them to apprehensively expect this emphasis to be a distraction from the pursuit of holiness and the work of the ministry.

I found that among this group there were a lot of misunderstandings about the love of God. I also found that many felt they already knew everything they needed to know about His love. To the surprise of both students and staff, by the end of the trimester their reservations were overcome, questions were answered, paradigms were altered, and lives were changed.

Like those students, many people carry misconceptions about the nature of God's love for them. Sometimes our spiritual experience is way ahead of our doctrinal understanding. Yet, our experience is interpreted by what we understand to be true. Many of us have systems of thought that block us from entering into a true encounter with God's love. Others entertain convictions that cut them off from deriving the full benefit of their intuitive exchanges with God.

This book will help you establish a solid foundation for relating to God on the basis of His love. Part of this process will be coming to terms with where our views of His love have been incorrect, and have thereby kept us from the fullness of the relationship He desires, and for which we were created. Establishing the right foundation can only take place through becoming exposed to a Biblically-based theology of God's love. In this book we will examine the Old and New Testaments, the viewpoints of the Apostles, and Jesus' example and testimony. We will establish a Biblical definition of love and through Scripture determine what God's love for us is like. We will endeavor to provide an answer to the question: Why does God love us?

Our goal is to bring you into a knowledge of Scripture which will lead to faith – faith which is meant to shape your worldview and lead to spiritual experience. The primary assertion of this book is that God loves each of us deeply, sincerely, and personally, and it is His desire for us to live in an ongoing experiential awareness of this love: to abide in the love of God. Our goal is to guide you towards this end.

As you read, maintain a hungry attitude towards God and a thoughtful attitude towards this material. Be like those who "received the word with great eagerness, examining the Scriptures daily to see whether these things were so" (Acts 17:11). While convinced that what is written here is essentially true, we recognize that, at best, it can only be part of the truth. "For we know in part and we prophesy in part" (1 Corinthians 13:9).

Yet, despite our limitations, we seek to imitate the attitude Paul exemplified: "But having the same spirit of faith, according to what is written, 'I believed, therefore I spoke,' we also believe, therefore we also speak" (2 Corinthians 4:13). As Peter and John testified, "We cannot stop speaking about what we have seen and heard" (Acts 4:20). So, in the spirit of faith, arrested by the love of God, believing that we are bearing witness to the testimony of the Spirit and the Scriptures, we commend this material to you.

Although you will be interacting with written materials, it is vital that you integrate the information and exhortation with your daily walk with God. To really benefit from this study, you need to be in contact with Him. What you read will inform your mind, but only an encounter with the Spirit of God can truly change your heart.

Before you begin, make a choice to meditate on the Word, pray through Scripture, and spend time in the presence of God. Our desire is that everyone who is reading this book will be working towards life change. We hope and pray that God would grant you the power to grasp His love for you, and that your relationship with God would be changed as you are faithful to maintain that grace. The outcome should be growth in your relationship with God, fresh confidence in Him, and a firm understanding of His love. Ultimately, knowing the love of God will lead to the release of the fullness of God (Ephesians 3:19). You may confidently expect that growing in your knowledge of God's love will benefit your life and affect your ministry for the better. Dive in with excitement and determination to receive all that God has for you; after all, you are God's true love!

# PART 1:

# RESTORING
# A BIBLICAL
# PERSPECTIVE

*The more I study the New Testament and live the Christian life, the more convinced I am that our fundamental difficulty, our fundamental lack, is the lack of seeing the love of God. It is not so much our knowledge that is defective but our vision of the love of God. Thus our greatest object and endeavor should be to know Him better, and thus we will love Him more truly.*

MARTIN LLOYD-JONES, *The Love of God*

*Love is absolutely central to our understanding of God.*

LEON MORRIS, *New Testament Theology*

*The Bible teaches that "God is love" and that God loves you. Nothing else matters so much.*

BILLY GRAHAM

*I never knew up to that time that God loved us so much. This heart of mine began to thaw out: I could not keep back the tears. I just drank it in…I tell you there is one thing that draws above everything else in the world and that is love.*

D.L. MOODY

*God pursues us to give us himself.*

JOHN WHITE, *God's Pursuing Love*

*It becomes clear that the sort of intimate union Jesus promises the disciples is not merely a mystical experience, but a relational encounter, for he gives it content with the term "love" (John 15:9–10).*

CRAIG S. KEENER, *The Gospel of John Volume II*

## Chapter 1

# Jesus, the Beloved Son

*Just as the Father has loved Me, I have also loved you. Abide in My love (John 15:9).*

LET'S BEGIN WITH A FEW QUESTIONS: How important is knowing the love of God? Is concentrating upon knowing God's love a subtle distraction from what really counts, or is this vital to the spiritual life of the believer? Is it valid to pursue knowledge of this love, or is it a waste of time?

To determine how significant the love of God is supposed to be in the life of a believer, we need to let Scripture inform and direct us. Let's answer these questions by asking another, better question: "What do the Scriptures teach about the importance of knowing God's love?"

As we look at Scripture, you will see that the Bible teaches: (1) knowing the love of God is important, (2) it is for every believer, and (3) it is supposed to be foundational to knowing God.

## Jesus' Example

If you scan the Gospels you will note that Jesus lived in an ongoing awareness of His Father's love. Jesus was very confident in His relationship with the Father. He knew that the Father cared for Him. He trusted in the Father. He entrusted Himself to the Father from the beginning to the end of His life (Psalm 71:6).

Let's look at a few clues the Scriptures give us about Their loving relationship. The heavenly Father communicated His affirmation and love for His Son at various times. At Jesus' immersion, He heard the voice of God. Father spoke directly to Jesus of His love:

> You are My beloved Son, in You I am well-pleased (Mark 1:11).

The Greek word which is translated "well-pleased" is *eudokia*. It is a strong word meaning *really pleased*, or *delighted*. Father's voice shattered the silent heavens as He declared how much He loved His Son. This formed Jesus' self image. This word branded His soul and provided self-definition, providing the foundation of the Messiah's inner awareness. This message from Father fortified Him against the devil's temptations and marked the future course of Jesus' ministry.

At His transfiguration the Father spoke of His love for Jesus to others. The Son was a witness to His Father's attestation:

> Then a cloud formed, overshadowing them, and a voice came out of the cloud, "This is My beloved Son, listen to Him!" (Mark 9:7).

Jesus spoke about the love that He experienced; He knew that the Father loved Him:

> Just as the Father has loved Me, I have also loved you; abide in My love (John 15:9).

He also knew why He was loved. He understood what it was about Him that the Father appreciated and esteemed. The Lamb of God knew why God was "well-pleased."

> For this reason the Father loves Me, because I lay down My life so that I may take it again (John 10:17).

The Scriptures testify that the Father entrusted all things to the Son. Why? Jesus testified of John the Baptist that not only was he a prophet, he was "more than a prophet" (Matthew 11:9). John's prophetic insight provided this answer: Jesus had authority because of His Father's love:

> The Father loves the Son and has given all things into His hand (John 3:35).

How much authority had the Father given Jesus? In the Gospel of John one need look no further than when He raised His voice and commanded, "Lazarus come forth!" John the Baptist's testimony was confirmed in John 13:3 where the apostle described the inner awareness of the Messiah: Jesus knew "that the Father had given all things into His hands."

The Messiah Jesus was viewed as a prophet who was on the same level as Moses (Acts 7:37; John 1:17). We have seen that John the Baptist understood Jesus' authority as originating in the Father's love. In the same way, the Son of God did not attribute His own prophetic insight to His holiness or His devotion to the God of Israel. The Messiah knew that He received revelation because of His Father's love for Him:

> For the Father loves the Son, and shows Him all things that He Himself is doing; and the Father will show Him greater works than these so that you will marvel (John 5:20).

As a result of knowing His Father's love, Jesus was supremely confident. Look at His boldness displayed even in the face of death:

> I knew that You always hear Me; but because of the people standing around I said it, so that they may believe that You sent Me (John 11:42).

Jesus thoroughly knew the reality of this love. He knew it well enough to pass on the same quality of love to His disciples. The experience He received was an experience the Messiah could give to others:

> Just as the Father has loved Me, I have also loved you (John 15:9a).

Immediately after Jesus washed His disciples' feet, He told them that He had given them a metaphor for their attitude and behavior. Then the Messiah told His disciples to love one another as He loved them. The truth of Jesus being our example was embraced by the Apostles. Peter exhorted us to "follow in His steps" (1 Peter 2:21). Paul told us to imitate his example just like he imitated Jesus (1 Corinthians 11:1). John expected the believers to purify themselves "as He (Jesus) is pure" (1 John 3:3). He wrote that as Jesus is, so are we in the world (1 John 4:17).

Many who read this will remember that John distinguished himself as the disciple who rested on Jesus' bosom. In this description there is a hint of Jesus' relationship to the Father. The same essential language is used to describe Jesus. He was called "the only begotten God who is in the bosom of the Father" (John 1:18). In that prophetic declaration we have a picture of the Messiah resting upon the breast of God. What a picture this is. What a depiction of intimacy and reliance. Jesus knew the Father's love. He rested upon God's heart. We are to do the same. After all, He has told us that His relationship to Father is the pattern of our relationship to Him.

The Messiah really is our example in all things. Our ultimate destiny is to be conformed to the image of God's Son (Romans 8:29). The sanctification process in which we participate is one aspect of the beginning of that glorification. It is amazing; this intimacy is both integral to our arriving at our ultimate destination, and the absolute goal of our sanctification.

Through these verses and others, we see that Jesus, our example in all things, knew the love of God as part of His normal and ongoing experience as a man. Since we are to follow His example we can be confident that our normal life is also supposed to include knowing and relying upon the love of God.

## Jesus' Commandment

Not only did our example, Jesus, personally live in an awareness of His Father's love, He also gave His disciples a commandment to do the same. Did you know you are commanded to know the love of God? It's true! Please read the following Scriptures to provide some context.

> I am the true vine, and My Father is the vinedresser. Every branch in Me that does not bear fruit, He takes away; and every branch that bears fruit, He prunes it, that it may bear more fruit. You are already clean because of the word which I have spoken to you. Abide in Me, and I in you. As the branch cannot bear fruit of itself, unless it abides in the vine, so neither can you, unless you abide in Me. I am the vine, you are the branches; he who abides in Me, and I in him, he bears much fruit; for apart from Me you can do nothing. If anyone does not abide in Me, he is thrown away as a branch, and dries up; and they gather them, and cast them into the fire, and they are burned. If you abide in Me, and My words abide in you, ask whatever you wish, and it shall be done for you. By this is My Father glorified, that you bear much fruit, and so prove to be My disciples (John 15:1–8).

When Jesus spoke these words, He was about to leave His disciples (John 13:1–3). He was giving them last-minute instructions, communicating what He wanted them to remember. What He said to them in His final hours with them is very important. This section of Scripture shows Jesus stressing a priority to His disciples. He wanted to impart what was closest to His heart. What was His priority? "Abide in Me."

The Messiah Jesus wanted His disciples to determine to stay in a vital union with Himself. He was about to return to Father and wanted the Apostles to prioritize keeping their relationship with Him alive. Jesus did not want their relationship with Him to end when He was no longer physically present. He wanted to maintain

His relationship to them. So Messiah told them: abide in Me, dwell in Me, live in Me, stay connected to Me, don't stop being with Me.

This word "abide" translates a Greek verb, *menein*. *Menein* means to remain, to dwell, to stay in one place for a period of time, to endure. It is also used to encourage people to wait. So *menein* can be translated: to live in, to stay in an attitude or activity of waiting. *Menein* is used to describe something which is enduring. The word is used 120 times in the New Testament and forty of those times (in thirty-three verses) are in John's Gospel. In 1 John the author uses *menein* twenty-four times (in eighteen verses). John speaks of the believer abiding in Jesus and Jesus dwelling in the believer. In John 15, both remaining in and maintaining an enduring relationship with Jesus are implied.

Many people embrace this commandment to abide in Jesus and then stop after these eight verses. Yet in the very next verse, Jesus gives us the key to abiding in Him: *Abiding in Me is abiding in My love for you.*

> **Just as the Father has loved Me, I have also loved you; abide in My love (John 15:9).**

It is not straining the meaning of this text to paraphrase it like this: "In the same way I know My Father's love, so I want you to remain in a conscious awareness of My love for you." There are a few consequential things here. Notice: This key is also a command. First, Jesus commands the disciples to abide in Him. Then He explains how, by giving them further direction in another commandment: "Stay in My love (and you will stay in Me)." You may never have read this passage in this way, but John wrote in such a way that these two commandments cannot be separated; they are linked together. We need to obey both commandments, yet obeying one is key to fulfilling the other.

The Messiah commanded us to abide in His love because it is important to God that we do this. He loves us and He wants us to know His love. Also notice: "As the Father has loved Me, I have also loved you." In remaining in Jesus' love, we not only have the key to maintaining a relationship with Him, but we also get to experience the same type of love that Jesus received from His Father. It is the same dynamic, powerful quality of love. This is an extraordinary love in which we are being commanded to abide (1 John 3:1). Remember, Jesus dwelled in His Father (John 1:18). We are receiving this instruction from the Master Abider. Jesus remained in a conscious awareness of His Father's love (John 5:20; 15:10). This was such a vital part of His life that He wanted His disciples (whom He loved) to do the same.

> If you keep My commandments, you will abide in My love, just as I have kept My Father's commandments and abide in His love (John 15:10).

Jesus has commanded us to abide in His love. This is the entry to, and substance of, abiding in Jesus. He wants us to do this. As we obey this command we build our relationship with Jesus on His terms, not ours.

## Chapter Summary

Let's recap: First we looked at the love of God in Jesus' life as an example for our relationship with God. We found that knowing the Father's love was a normal and ongoing part of Jesus' life. He understood and experienced His Father's love. It was a reality to Him. As this is true of Jesus, it is to be true of us as well.

Next, we saw that Jesus gave His disciples a commandment to abide in Him. He gave them the key to maintaining this relationship with Himself: by giving them a command to abide in His love. Because it is a commandment, we know that it's important to Jesus. It was given to people who would no longer have Messiah's physical presence. If it was valid for them, it is valid for us. The Lord wants us to live in the same way He lived. Jesus dwelled in His Father's love and wants us to know His love in the same way. Both His life and His teachings illustrate that knowing the love of God is normative and vital. Abiding in the love of God is a key to abiding in and relating to Jesus.

## Consider

God told Moses to build the tabernacle on the earth according to the pattern of what he saw in heaven:

> Let them construct a sanctuary for Me, that I may dwell among them. According to all that I am going to show you, as the pattern of the tabernacle and the pattern of all its furniture, just so you shall construct it (Exodus 25:8–9).

Taking this instruction as a prophetic paradigm, we see that we are to build our relationship with Him according to the pattern He establishes. We want to give ourselves to Him. We are taking the role of subjects, students, servants. Might we not say, "Lord, You establish the relationship just the way You want it to be." After all, He is God. He has established relationships with people before us. He has all the experience. He knows what He is doing.

We ask, "How shall I build this relationship with You, Lord?" and He replies, "Just as the Father has loved Me, I have also loved you; abide in My love." This is a crucial part of His pattern. This is a significant aspect of His blueprint for my life and yours. How are you building? Are you abiding in His love?

1.  What was the most important truth you learned from this chapter?

2.  List three verses that indicate that God wants you to know and abide in His love.

3.  Jesus is our example. Spend time considering what the Gospels teach about Jesus' relationship with His Father. What does this tell you about the relationship God desires to have with you?

4. Have you ever considered John 15:9 as a commandment? Does knowing this is a commandment affect your walk with God? How so?

5. What do you think abiding in Jesus' love looks like in the life of a believer?

6. What did you struggle with the most in this chapter? Consider taking further time to study the Scriptures about this topic, and commit it to prayer.

7. Please paraphrase, personalize and pray through John 15:9:

> Just as the Father has loved Me, I have also loved you. Abide in My love.

*A correct belief means an acceptance of the apostolic witness and testimony.*

MARTIN LLOYD-JONES, *The Love of God*

*God has no favorites, except as some of His children by their loving response make it possible for Him to shower more love upon them.*

A. W. TOZER

*Everyone is God's favorite, but not everybody knows it.*

ROBIN MCMILLAN

*When Jesus died on the cross, He was giving "all He had" to pay the price for all the wrong things you've ever done. In your heart, for just a moment, would you walk up that hill the Bible calls Skull Hill and stand quietly at the foot of that cross where the Son of God is pouring out His life for you. Look at Him dying for you! You are not worthless!*

RON HUTCHCRAFT

*Avail yourself of the greatest privilege this side of heaven. Jesus Christ died to make this communion and communication with the Father possible.*

BILLY GRAHAM

## Chapter 2

# Witnesses from the Inner Circle

*For Christ also died for sins once for all, the just for the*
*unjust, so that He might bring us to God (1 Peter 3:18a).*

SCRIPTURE TEACHES THAT on the evidence of two or three witnesses
a matter shall be confirmed (Deuteronomy 19:15). We have just
looked at Jesus' example of living in an ongoing awareness of the
Father's love. We have seen that Jesus commands us, as His disciples, to follow His example and abide in His love. Let's look at a
few other key witnesses in Scripture.

Within the circle of Jesus' disciples, there was another circle of
those whom He appointed as Apostles (the Twelve). Within the
circle of Apostles was yet another circle. Some have referred to this
as the inner circle, those Apostles who were closest to Jesus and
were most frequently named and involved in the Gospel narratives.
Often, we find these same three men called out by Jesus: Peter,
James, and John.

It is no surprise then that we find in the writings of Peter and John
a common thread of God's love for humanity. These men were
closer to Jesus than any others in their day and, having learned well,
they integrated Jesus' teachings into their lives and ministries. Let's
briefly examine how John and Peter related to God's love.

## John's Example

By the end of the first century, the material contained in the Synoptic Gospels was dispersed throughout the Church. John was aware of what the Church knew and he wrote in the light of that knowledge. This Apostle gave us both narrative and instruction that complements and yet is often very different from what the Church had already received. John wanted to make sure certain things were not overlooked or forgotten. He wanted us to have a fuller vision of Jesus' teaching, so he communicated what he found to be most important, most needful for the Church. This Apostle also sought to reveal what was most significant to him.

John alone recorded the commandment to abide in Jesus' love; none of the Synoptics document this statute. What does that say about John's appreciation of this edict's value? We know that he took love seriously. An examination of 1 John shows that out of 105 verses the word "love" is used thirty times (in twenty-six verses). That's a little more than one out of every four verses. John is saying "God is love" and "love one another" a lot!

It is evident that he took the command to abide in the love of Jesus to heart. Why else is there a John 3:16 without a corresponding Matthew, Mark, and Luke "3:16"? The Apostle John took God's love very seriously.

Remember, at the time this Gospel was written, John was the only surviving member of the Twelve Apostles. He had outlived all of his peers. The Spirit had more time to work on him than with any of the other writers of the New Testament. He lived throughout most of the first century and wrote this Gospel towards the end of his life. Every foundation upon which a natural man rests was gone. His parents were gone, his brother was gone, his best friends and co-laborers were gone, his best hopes for the return of the Lord in his lifetime were dashed with the destruction of Jerusalem. The nature of the Church had changed, becoming more institutional and non-Jewish by the decade. He was displaced, living as a cultural alien in Asia Minor. Being elderly, John was also out of his own time. Such a one sees things from a perspective that is different from those around him.

In addition, John probably knew Jesus better than any other person on the planet. He had talked with Jesus, eaten with Jesus, followed Jesus, and listened to Jesus. John was with Jesus at the Transfiguration and at Gethsemane; he knew Jesus when He was feasting with friends and when He was overturning tables at the Temple. He had walked with Jesus, and their feet carried dirt from the same road. John was present at the cross and a witness of Messiah's resurrection. John *knew* Jesus.

Now we are getting a clearer picture of John. He's one of the Twelve – the only one left. He was the Apostle who received the Revelation of Jesus concerning what was and is and what is to come. Consider this: John was the type of man to whom that Revelation *could* be given. John was truly an awesome man of God. Yet, how does he refer to himself in his Gospel? Does he say, "I am John, one of the Twelve. I know Him the best of all." Or perhaps, "I am John, the most spiritually significant man alive today." No, John doesn't even write his name! Let's look at what John wrote of himself at the height of his self-disclosure:

> There was reclining on Jesus' bosom, one of the disciples, whom Jesus loved (John 13:23).
>
> Jesus then saw His mother and the disciple He loved standing nearby and said to His mother, "Woman, behold your son" (John 19:26).
>
> So she ran to Simon Peter and to the other disciple whom Jesus loved, and said to them, "They have taken away our Lord" (John 20:2).
>
> Therefore that disciple, whom Jesus loved, said to Peter, "It is the Lord" (John 21:7).

> Then Peter, turning around, saw the disciple whom Jesus loved following them, the one who had leaned back on His bosom at the supper, and said, "Lord, who is it that betrays you?" (John 21:20).

The reality of Jesus' personal love for each individual had been so received and internalized by John that it deeply affected his self-image. So much so, that he referred to himself as "the disciple whom Jesus loved." John lived the command to abide.

Let's consider again what this man had lived through. Think of the wild extremes of his experience within one weekend of his life. Just the trauma of Jesus' betrayal and crucifixion would be enough to scar a man's soul. The exhilaration of being a witness of His resurrection would correspondingly produce an indelible mark upon his life: one that would shape the totality of his future.

In addition, reconsider the reality John understood about himself. Imagine the temptation to elitism and authoritarianism that could assail John. He knew he had more spiritual authority than anyone else on earth. John knew, as one of the Twelve, that his testimony had the potential to be the most impacting message of his time. This is a man who instructed the "fathers" of the Church as if they were his grandchildren. What type of revelation is required to preserve a man from the pride of being the foremost spiritual authority on the planet?

John was consumed with the fire of eternal life. He knew the God who is love. He both knew and meditated upon the love of Jesus to the degree that to this day he is known as the disciple whom Jesus loved. The love of Jesus made such an impression on his life that he was passionately committed to getting out the message of the love of God. John was familiar with the information in the Synoptic Gospels. After all, he was a witness! Yet when he chose to write his testimony, he brought out a different emphasis.

When we read the Gospel of John, we're getting to sit at the feet of this man who knew Jesus in an incredibly deep, intimate, and personal way. Let's ask the writer of the Gospel some questions.

"What's your name?"

*It's not important.*

"What office are you walking in?"

*It's not important.*

"What's your ethnic background?"

*It's not important.*

"Well, you're frustrating me. What is important?"

*I'll tell you what has kept me my entire life. Jesus loves me. Jesus loves me, that is what has kept me. That's what's going on here. I'm the disciple whom Jesus loved.*

What is the most powerful theological treatise, profound key, or earth-shattering truth to the man who knew Jesus better than anyone on the planet? The content is found in a children's song: "Jesus loves me, this I know."

## Peter's Testimony

Though the Scriptures only contain two short letters from Peter, he is mentioned in the New Testament almost as frequently as Paul. Peter is widely held to have been the most influential leader among the Twelve Apostles post crucifixion and resurrection. He was a pivotal man in the early history of the Church.

In examining Peter's perspective of the love of God, we're going to begin by going back to Peter's relationship with the Man, Jesus. The recorded testimony of Peter's discipleship reveals an inconsistent man at best. Peter walked on water; Peter was called Satan by Jesus.

Peter had the pivotal revelation and confession of Jesus as the Messiah; Peter denied Jesus three times. The written record reveals that Peter was a real human being with ups and downs in his walk with God.

Peter, then, provides a glimpse into Jesus' heart towards all who betray Him. We know that he received remarkable direct revelation from the Father. We know he was one of the closest Apostles to Jesus. Yet, Peter, this "rock" in his Master's hour of need, not only left Him (as the other disciples did), but also perjured himself as he denied the Messiah. Let's look at Matthew's account of Peter's betrayal:

> But he denied it before them all, saying, "I do not know what you are talking about" (Matthew 26:70).

> And again he denied it with an oath, "I do not know the man" (Matthew 26:72).

> Then he began to curse and swear, "I do not know the man!" And immediately a rooster crowed (Matthew 26:74).

This must have been intensely traumatic for Peter. I wonder whether he was aware during this process that he was failing. The pressure on his soul must have been immense. These verses from Luke 22 are almost heartbreakingly painful to even consider:

> The Lord turned and looked at Peter and Peter remembered the word of the Lord, how He had told him, "Before a rooster crows today, you will deny Me three times." And he went out and wept bitterly (Luke 22:61–62).

Time passed between the betrayal and the reconciliation. Peter had to live with himself and what he had done. I'm sure his shockingly reflexive denial of Jesus was on Peter's mind as the Messiah Jesus was flogged and crucified. I'm sure it was on his mind when Jesus rose three days later, and every day after that, until Jesus healed the breach.

What must it have felt like to be in Peter's shoes? How would it feel to brag that you will never leave the Master, never fail to stand with

Him, even unto death, and then to reflexively do the very thing you have sworn not to do? What must his heart have felt like in that moment when Jesus turned and looked at him? Devastation, utter brokenness, even self-loathing must have been Peter's experience in the following days. Thankfully, this is not the end of this history. Let's turn to John's Gospel for the resolution of the story.

> So when they had finished breakfast, Jesus said to Simon Peter, "Simon, son of John, do you love Me more than these?" He said to Him, "Yes, Lord; You know that I love You." He said to him, "Tend My lambs."
>
> He said to him again a second time, "Simon, son of John, do you love Me?" He said to Him, "Yes, Lord; You know that I love You." He said to him, "Shepherd My sheep."
>
> He said to him the third time, "Simon, son of John, do you love Me?" Peter was grieved because He said to him the third time, "Do you love Me?" And he said to Him, "Lord, You know all things; You know that I love You." Jesus said to him, "Tend My sheep" (John 21:15–17).

Some contend that this passage shows Jesus bringing Peter to the end of himself in a deeper way. This element could certainly be present. The text itself says that Peter was pained that Jesus asked him a third time if he loved Him. Yet, it is obvious that Jesus was motivated to help Peter enter into restored fellowship with Himself and to reaffirm Peter's calling and destiny. His questions to Peter were searching, but Jesus knew the answer. Was He asking for His own good or for Peter's good? Perhaps Peter needed to hear the answer to these questions from his own lips. Perhaps he needed to come to the realization that he did indeed love Jesus. Perhaps he needed to be assured that there was something in him, something rocklike, from which he might go forward in serving Jesus. Seen in this light, the Messiah was not shattering Peter; He was gently and firmly leading him back to Himself. The Lord confirmed Peter's calling. He reassured him that he still had a role to play. Jesus firmly put the past in the past, and called Peter to look to the future. He fully restored this broken, tortured soul.

This experience must have been something that Peter held onto for the rest of his life. Peter, after denying his Lord, was still an Apostle, still belonged to Jesus, and still had a "place." He was not utterly cast out, not written off as worthless by Jesus. The risen Messiah lovingly brought Peter from a terrible depth to a wonderful height. What an extraordinary experience!

Jesus told a parable that is relevant to Peter's experience of the Lord's forgiveness:

> Two men owed money to a certain moneylender. One owed him five hundred denarii, and the other fifty. Neither of them had the money to pay him back, so he canceled the debts of both. Now which of them will love him more?
>
> Simon (not Peter) replied, "I suppose the one who had the bigger debt canceled."
>
> "You have judged correctly," Jesus said (Luke 7:41–43).

Having had such a tremendous debt canceled, Peter must have loved Jesus all the more deeply. No doubt, he must have appreciated the love that Jesus had – the wonderful, forgiving, merciful, welcoming love of Jesus – in an exceptionally deep way. So deeply, in fact, that it became the foundation upon which the rest of his life and service was built. Without the love of Jesus, Peter's story might have ended with his return to fishing. Could he have gone on ministering in the name of the Lord whom he had betrayed, without the restoring demonstration of His forgiving love, without the renewed call to serve Him? To understand Peter's personal perspective of the love of God, we need look no further than Peter's denial and restoration. If any man knew the healing, forgiving, restoring, welcoming love of God, it was this man.

## Peter's Writings

What about Peter's writings? What does he tell us about the love of God? In contrast to John's writings, the love of God is specifically mentioned only a few times in Peter's letters. And yet, his writings are infused with his understanding of the foundational nature of God's love.

One of the major themes of Peter's writings is the covenant relationship between God and His people, as seen in the Hebrew Scriptures. Peter relies heavily on the Old Testament as he writes. He speaks of our relationship with God through Jesus with a frame of reference similar to that of the Old Testament authors. Sometimes Peter quotes the Torah and the Prophets. Why this heavy reliance?

For starters, Peter was a Jewish man. Peter's view of redemption was shaped by the sacred Hebrew Scriptures, the record of Israel's history, in particular the record of the Exodus. Every Jewish family was commanded to remember and commemorate the Exodus (Exodus 12:14). Peter had been steeped in this history from childhood. As a child he had heard the story recited over and over. Later, when he had his own household, Peter would retell the tale. It is no wonder it shaped his understanding of our redemption.

Beyond this, however, Peter was writing with a purpose; he had a point he wanted to make. One thing he wanted to get across was the wondrous nature of what God has done for us, of what He has in store for us, of His heart towards us. The Exodus was a familiar story, firmly established as sacred history. It provided Peter with a revelatory pattern from which to draw frequent illustrations.

Let's consider for a few moments what this Exodus language in Peter means. First of all, the Exodus is a story of redemption. It reveals a pattern of how God works in the lives of individuals and groups. The Exodus is Israel's history, yet it reveals God's plans for every man; it reveals God's plans for you. Though Peter doesn't spell out the love of God, certainly, His love is revealed in the Exodus.

## Redemption: It's Personal

It is easy to take the following concept for granted, but it is vital to remember that God is very personally invested in the process of redemption.

Look at what God said to Moses in Exodus 3:7–8a. Notice how personal this is:

> The LORD said, "I have surely seen the affliction of My people who are in Egypt, and have given heed to their cry because of their task-masters, for I am aware of their sufferings. So I have come down to deliver them from the power of the Egyptians, and to bring them up from that land to a good and spacious land, to a land flowing with milk and honey."

"I have surely seen" – not, "I have heard a report." God Himself saw them.

"…the affliction of *My* people" – not, "an oppressed people, and I have a principled ethical hatred of oppression." "*My* people" – these people belonged to God.

"I…have given heed…I am aware" – God was personally responding to their cries for deliverance.

"I have come down…to deliver…to bring them up" – God Himself came down to accomplish His delightful purposes for them – "to bring them up from that land to a good and spacious land." This land was the location of God's "holy habitation," this was the place He had chosen to dwell, His very own land (Exodus 15:13).

This same personal involvement is mirrored in 1 Peter 1:3:

> Blessed be the God and Father of our Lord Jesus Christ, who according to His great mercy has caused us to be born again to a living hope through the resurrection of Jesus Christ from the dead.

As God personally redeemed Israel, God Himself redeems us in the person of His very own Son. We should receive this deeply, personally. In the same way God guided Israel to His dwelling place, we are being brought into a present and eternal fellowship with Him.

Let's take a deeper look at the level of God's personal investment in our redemption.

The God of Israel gave His people specific instructions concerning the first Passover. The plan was the same for large families and for small. If the firstborn of each household was to be saved, if God was to protectively hover over each household, then one primary thing was needed: the blood of a spotless young lamb.

Like Israel, we all need redemption. We too need the blood of a Lamb. We are enslaved to selfishness, sin, the world system, and satanic powers. An atoning sacrifice for sin is absolutely necessary, and it can only be found through the shed blood of the Messiah, Jesus.

> You were not redeemed with perishable things like silver or gold from your futile way of life inherited from your forefathers, but with precious blood, as of a lamb unblemished and spotless, the blood of Christ (1 Peter 1:18–19).

## Redemption: The Price Equals the Value

Peter pronounced the blood of Jesus to be "precious" (1 Peter 1:19). This is important. Please consider this: our worth to the Creator is demonstrated by the ransom He paid – the Lamb's precious blood, the blood of His beloved Son. God loved you enough to offer up His only Son as a sacrifice for your sins. Nothing is more valuable than the blood of Jesus. This uttermost price indicates your absolute value to God, the degree of our indebtedness, and the ruthlessly loving determination of God to redeem us.

Only the precious blood of Jesus is valuable enough to pay the high price for our redemption. Psalm 49:7–8 tells us: "No man can redeem the life of another or give to God a ransom for him – the ransom for a life is costly, no payment is ever enough." The blood of Jesus is the only worthy ransom. As we consider this, we can begin to rightly esteem the value of the Messiah's blood. When we see what God was willing to pay, we are able to appreciate what we are worth to Him. Again, this extraordinary price indicates the astonishingly high value God places upon you.

In paying such a price, was He deceived? Did He pay a high price for what is essentially valueless? Perhaps in our own estimation we would say, "Yes." However, in this instance, faith triumphs over the voice of reason. We must bow our evaluations and recognize that we are invaluable to the Father. How valuable? Well, how precious is the blood of the beloved Son of God?

## Redemption: The Reason

In the light of God's personal involvement in our redemption, let's ask Peter a question: "Peter, why did Jesus die for me?" Note his answer:

> For Christ also died for sins once for all, the just for the unjust, so that He might bring us to God (1 Peter 3:18a).

Why did He die? Was it because He hates you? Is He indifferent? No, Jesus loves you and wants you to be with Him where He is. Jesus is in the Father's presence. He is where the Father dwells. Jesus gave up His life to bring you to God. Messiah atoned for you so you could abide with God. He died to draw you to Father.

Once again, Peter refers his readers to the Exodus event. He's utilizing the same type of language used to describe Israel's deliverance from Egypt.

> Thus says the LORD, "Let My people go, that they may (worship) Me" (Exodus 8:1b).

> In Your lovingkindness You have led the people whom You have re-
> deemed; In Your strength You have guided them to Your holy habita-
> tion (Exodus 15:13).

> You will bring them and plant them in the mountain of Your inherit-
> ance, The place, O LORD, which You have made for Your dwelling, The
> sanctuary, O Lord, which Your hands have established (Exodus 15:17).

> But you shall seek the LORD at the place which the LORD your God
> will choose from all your tribes, to establish His name there for His
> dwelling, and there you shall come (Deuteronomy 12:5).

God's desire for humanity to be with Him is hinted at from the
beginning of Israel's history. The purpose of redemption and their
settling the Land was that they might live with God at the center of
their lives. God redeemed Israel to guide them to the place He chose
to dwell. According to Peter, we should receive this as a holy proto-
type because this is also God's pattern for us! This is God's motivation, this is why Jesus died for us; He did it to bring us to God. Why?
Because of God's desire and love for us. This is Peter's gospel.

## Chapter Summary

When we looked at the way John related to the love of God, we
found that he personally embraced and deeply received the love of
God. His identity was fundamentally shaped by the love of God;
his identity could not be separated from the love that Jesus had for
him. This is a profound example of abiding in the love of Jesus. It
is easy to see that, to John, knowing the love of God was an important part of his reality and relationship with God. His writings overflow with the love of God. He wanted to pass the knowledge of
this love along.

We know that Peter's personal relationship with Jesus was also
shaped by Jesus' love. After he denied the Messiah, Jesus restored
him. Consequently, Peter's life was marked by the loving acceptance, restoration, and forgiveness of Jesus. We can also see that to

Simon bar Jonah, the love of God was a rock-like reality. At the center of Peter's understanding of redemption was the Exodus, and the Exodus clearly displays the loving heart of God towards His people, Israel. To Peter, we too are being personally "brought out" by a loving faithful Deliverer. To Peter, the love of God is woven deeply into the story of our redemption.

From these two men we once again find that the love of God is supposed to be central to the life of a believer. The story of redemption, the forgiveness of God, Jesus' death on the cross, all of these things are pointing towards the loving heart of God.

## Consider

Does God love some people more than others? Yes. Does God love everyone the same? Yes.

Imagine a row of glasses. Each of them is intended to "receive." Some, however, are already filled. Now imagine an inexhaustible, overwhelming supply of love that is waiting to be poured upon and into these vessels. The pouring is already taking place – but some are receiving more than others. Some vessels are full – anything poured into them spills over. Some are partially empty. A few are empty.

If God's love is being poured upon these vessels, which are being filled? Which are receiving? Which are rejecting? Is the same amount of love being poured onto each vessel? Yes. Is the same amount of love being received by each vessel? No.

Now, suppose God's love is not "static" but "dynamic" love…a love that knows, searches, interacts, delivers, strengthens. Suppose that *that* is what is being poured out. Then, are there vessels that are being "loved" more than others? Well, if the term "loved" is a dynamic verb indicating interaction, yes. But the same amount of love is available for each vessel. Each glass is under a continual outpouring of divine attention and compassion.

What type of vessel are you? Open up and receive.

1.  What is the most important truth you learned in this chapter?

2.  Based on what we have studied so far, is knowing the love of God supposed to be foundational in the life of a believer? Why or why not?

3.  Please read Exodus 19:4:

    > You yourselves have seen what I did to the Egyptians, and how I bore you on eagles' wings, and brought you to Myself.

    What is God's stated motive for redeeming the Israelites? Explain what this tells you about the motives for God's activity in your life?

4.  In Scripture, we see that John is uniquely aware of God's love for him. No other disciple or Apostle describes himself as John does. The tendency might be to think that John experienced a relationship with Jesus which is not available to everyone else. Do you see John's relationship with Jesus as something available to you? Why or why not? Is there Scripture which forms your perspective?

5.  What did you struggle with the most in this chapter? Consider taking further time to study the Scriptures about this topic, and commit it to prayer.

6.  Please paraphrase, personalize and pray through 1 Peter 3:18a:

    > For Christ also died for sins once for all, the just for the unjust, so that He might bring us to God.

*All my life I've been searching for that crazy missing part*

*And with one touch, You just rolled away the stone that held my heart*

*And now I see that the answer was as easy, as just asking You in*

*And I am so sure I could never doubt Your gentle touch again*

*It's like the power of the wind*

*Like waking up from the longest dream, how real it seemed*

*Until Your love broke through*

*I've been lost in a fantasy, that blinded me*

*Until Your love, until Your love, broke through*

KEITH GREEN, RANDY STONEHILL

*Herein was manifested the love of God, that God sent His only begotten Son to death, to the cruel shame and agony and suffering of the cross, to be made sin for us who Himself knew no sin and so was innocent.*

MARTIN LLOYD-JONES, *The Love of God*

*There is an experience of the love of God which, when it comes upon us, and enfolds us, and bathes us, and warms us, is so utterly new that we can hardly identify it with the old phrase, God is love. Can this be the love of God, this burning, tender, wooing, wounding pain of love that pierces the marrow of my bones and burns out old loves and ambitions? God experienced is a vast surprise.*

THOMAS R. KELLY

# Chapter 3

# Paul's Pattern

*The life I now live in the flesh I live by faith in the Son of God, who loved me and gave Himself up for me (Galatians 2:20b).*

NOW THAT WE HAVE EXAMINED the viewpoints of two of the Twelve Apostles, let's turn to the foremost writer of the New Testament Scriptures: Paul. The following are the first words Paul ever heard from Jesus:

Saul, Saul, why are you persecuting Me? (Acts 9:4b).

When Paul encountered Jesus, the glorified Son of Man expressed an intense identification with the believers. Paul had been persecuting the Church (Galatians 1:13), but the Lord revealed that Paul had actually been harassing the Messiah, Himself (Acts 22:7). The "radiance of (God's) glory and the exact representation of (God's) nature" (Hebrews 1:3a) confronted Paul, proclaiming His covenantal concern for the Church. When the Church is persecuted, Jesus takes it personally.

Jesus also revealed His personal concern for Paul. He interrupted Paul's course, preventing him from further sin, and immediately gave him instructions. When Paul obeyed them, it resulted in the revelation of a commission to represent the God of Israel to the Gentiles.

We recognize that all believers are to be examples to others (1 Thessalonians 1:6–7). Paul saw that as true about himself. For example, in 2 Thessalonians 3:7–9 Paul wrote:

> For you yourselves know how you ought to follow our example, because we did not act in an undisciplined manner among you, nor did we eat anyone's bread without paying for it, but with labor and hardship we kept working night and day so that we would not be a burden to any of you; not because we do not have the right to this, but in order to offer ourselves as a model for you, so that you would follow our example.

He also presented himself as an example in the same way other ancient moral teachers would to their disciples. Read Philippians 4:9:

> The things you have learned and received and heard and seen in me, practice these things, and the God of peace will be with you.

Yet Paul understood that, in a special way, his life was a pattern for the believer. Take a look at these verses:

> Yet for this reason I found mercy, so that in me as the foremost, Jesus Christ might demonstrate His perfect patience as an example for those who would believe in Him for eternal life (1 Timothy 1:16).

> Brethren, join in following my example, and observe those who walk according to the pattern you have in us (Philippians 3:17).

Paul served as a uniquely God-given pattern to the Gentile churches. As such, his testimony is very important to the Church throughout the nations.

We know that the mouth speaks out of the abundance of the heart (Luke 6:45). In the same way, people act according to their inner natures. When we get glimpses of Paul's inner life, we should pay attention. How did he view his relationship with Jesus? Paul's personal testimony concerning the love of God is found in Galatians 2:20b: "...the Son of God, who loved me and gave Himself up for me."

Notice that Paul radically personalized this love. Paul fully recognized and embraced God's love for him, the individual. He spoke of Jesus' sacrificial atoning death as if he were its focus, as if Jesus' death was personally accomplished just for Paul. We know, from the Biblical record, that Paul was nowhere around when Jesus was ministering. If it is true that Jesus knew and loved Paul, it is also true that He knows and loves you. If Paul could know the love of Jesus, so can you. He did know this love; it was definitely part of his personal understanding of redemption. This knowledge of Jesus' love is an important part of Paul's pattern and example for us. We should receive this example. We should conform our hearts to this pattern. Let's build our souls according to this inner blueprint.

## Objectively and Subjectively Knowing God's Love

Within his writings, Paul gives us additional perspective about knowing the love of God. To Paul, this love was more than mere information on a page. It was an absolutely demonstrated reality, an ongoing experience for the believer and a foundation for the exercise of faith.

To explore the theme of God's love in Paul's writings, it is helpful to use the terms "objective love" and "subjective love." Objective love is love which is established fact; love which can be seen by observers, love which is clearly demonstrated. Objective love is not recognized by spiritual sensation; it is known through the Scriptural record and testimony. This is a foundational form of love you may or may not "feel." It is love revealed by Biblical evidence and then embraced by faith. This assurance will affect our emotions, but this faith and its result is not the same thing as intuitively experiencing the love of which the Scriptures testify. Our text for demonstrating objective love is Romans 5:6–8:

> For while we were still helpless, at the right time the Messiah died for the ungodly. For one will hardly die for a righteous man; though perhaps for the good man someone would dare even to die. But

> God demonstrates His own love toward us, in that while we were
> yet sinners, Christ died for us.

Our other term is subjective love. This is the love we objectively
know exists, being made real by the Holy Spirit to our spiritual per-
ceptions. Paul referred to our capacity to experience spiritual perception when He prayed that the believers would have the eyes of their
hearts "enlightened, so that you will know…" (Ephesians 1:18). Subjective love is knowing God's love through spiritual experience. Subjective love is also prominent in Paul's writings. Our text for demonstrating subjective love is found earlier in Romans 5:1–5:

> Therefore having been justified by faith, we have peace with God
> through our Lord Jesus Christ, through whom also we have obtained
> our introduction by faith into this grace in which we stand; and we
> exult in hope of the glory of God. And not only this, but we also exult
> in our tribulations, knowing that tribulation brings about persever-
> ance; and perseverance, proven character; and proven character,
> hope; and hope does not disappoint, because the love of God has
> been poured out within our hearts through the Holy Spirit who was
> given to us.

In Paul's writings we discover that we are to know God's love both
objectively and subjectively. This knowledge requires faith. We decide to believe on the basis of evidence. Faith is the heart coming
into line with the objective evidence. Faith releases and opens the
door for the subjective experience of God's love, "for he who comes
to God must believe that He is and that He is a rewarder of those
who seek Him" (Hebrews 11:6b). This is similar to what John wrote
in 1 John 4:16a: "We have come to know and have believed the love
which God has for us."

Grasping the fundamental content of the objective revelation is
extremely important. It is not mere head knowledge. It must not be
seen as being in opposition to subjective knowledge. The message
of the love of God is to be highly honored. The truth of God's
love demonstrated at the cross is a treasure and must be highly

valued. Objective revelation is a source of stability and a means of access to spiritual reality. Romans 5:1–11 is representative of Paul's approach to the love of God. In this passage we find instruction about the subjective experience of God's love, the objective knowledge of God's love, and a resulting apostolic meditation.

Let's look at these elements again. In Romans 5:1–5 Paul writes about the experience of knowing God's love: "The love of God has been poured out within our hearts through the Holy Spirit who was given to us." He testifies about an experience, not a recollection of cognitive data. He referred the believers to their spiritual encounter with God's love which they held in common. This is a Pauline understanding of abiding in God's love: God's love should be experienced.

Reinforcing this subjective experience, Paul exhorted them upon the basis of the objective love of God:

> For while we were still helpless, at the right time Christ died for the ungodly. For one will hardly die for a righteous man; though perhaps for the good man someone would dare even to die. But God demonstrates His own love toward us, in that while we were yet sinners, Christ died for us (Romans 5:6–8).

This is exceptional instruction. *Believers are to objectively reflect upon the quality of Jesus' love.* How much does He love you? Remember, 1 Peter 3:18 informs us that Messiah died "that He might bring us to God." In the light of that, let's ask this: how much does God desire to bring you to Himself?

> But God demonstrates His own love toward us, in that while we were yet sinners, Christ died for us (Romans 5:8).

The word in Romans 5:8 translated "demonstrates" means to act in such a way as to prove something by way of analogy. (*Thayer's Greek Lexicon* defines *sunistemi* in this way – to put together by way of composition or combination, to teach by combining and comparing, hence, to show, prove, establish, exhibit. Here is *Louw & Nida's* definition: to make known by action, to demonstrate.) This type of demonstration can be seen in the disciplines of science and math. It is similar to the word "proves."

Through the incarnation God established that He longs for you enough to die for you. At the cross He revealed the full extent of His love to help you understand the depth of His desire. No one would die to obtain something they didn't treasure. This is evidence that He loves you and He wants you. This immense love is unmistakable, but (along with Paul) we're rehearsing this obvious truth because, to consistently abide in His love we must employ our faith.

Let's recognize and employ the following pattern: Paul first reminded the Romans of their common experience (His love has been poured out in your hearts). Then he called them to recall the objective evidence (He has proven His love for you at Calvary). This reminds us that if we are to consistently experience God's love we must activate our faith. By practicing this pattern, we will learn to abide in the love of God. You are fully able to abide in the love of God; you should.

## Enlightened Extrapolation

God sought to make how much He loves you *painfully* obvious. Remember, your value to God is measured by the price He was willing to pay to ransom you; your worth to the Creator has been proven by the price He paid. Consider the extent of this love in light of the fact that this passage describes our spiritual state as being God's "enemies."

Paul progresses from subjective experience to objective evidence. The apostle moves the readers from recalling their feelings to remembering the facts. Then he continues, encouraging believers to exercise their faith as they extrapolate from the evidence:

> Much more then, having now been justified by His blood, we shall be saved from the wrath of God through Him. For if while we were

enemies, we were reconciled to God through the death of His Son, much more, having been reconciled, we shall be saved by His life. And not only this, but we also exult in God through our Lord Jesus Christ, through whom we have now received the reconciliation (Romans 5:9–11).

This section of Scripture contains carefully measured conclusions. After having meditated upon their experience and the objective demonstration of God's love, Paul employed "sanctified thought" by drawing inferences from the evidence. Utilizing sanctified thought is part of abiding in God's love. It's part of making the evidence real to your intellect and imagination. The way you use your mind affects your heart. These faith-inspired convictions lead to the exercise of bold confidence in God and consequent acts of holy obedience. Here's an example of apostolic extrapolation:

For if while we were enemies we were reconciled through the death of His Son, how much more having been reconciled... (Romans 5:10)

Paul is meditating upon this love and drawing some logical conclusions. We're called to do the same. *The instruction is an example. The example is an instruction.* We are to consider the subjective and objective evidence. We are to fearlessly draw conclusions. Convicted of the truth, we are to exercise our faith and act upon what we believe.

Part of the abiding process is training your mind to think in line with what has been objectively revealed. It is called "conforming your mind to the truth." It is called "having your mind transformed" (John 8:31–32, Romans 12:2). The word comes. We receive it. We pray. We think about it. We agree. We apply (James 1:21b–22).

Paul consistently employs this pattern. He's constantly coming out with sanctified thought and imagination, for instance: "For perhaps he was for this reason separated from you for a while, that you would have him back forever" (Philemon 1:15).

Paul uses the word "perhaps" to say something like, "Who knows but maybe this happened for this specific reason." Paul's manner of thought invites us to respectfully speculate upon the basis of what we know God has revealed about Himself. We are not to be so presumptuous as to declare that we definitely know the reasons for various occurrences; even at the height of prophetic inspiration, we must embrace reality and confess that "we know in part and we prophesy in part" (1 Corinthians 13:9). Even though this is true, God invites us through the enscriptured apostolic example to form and share with others sanctified, faith-filled deductions.

Look carefully; here is an excellent example which is relevant to our topic:

> What then shall we say to these things? If God is for us, who is against us? He who did not spare His own Son, but delivered Him over for us all, how will He not also with Him freely give us all things? (Romans 8:31–32).

What a great conclusion! I'm glad it is in the Bible. Let's savor this sanctified thought: "He who did not spare His own Son but delivered Him over for us all, how will He not also, with Him, freely give us all things?"

Sanctified thought is illumined logic based upon revelation. It is the use of Holy Spirit enhanced reason which reinforces the objective of the original inspired revelation. This type of thought doesn't detract from the Word, it reinforces it.

> And He said to him, "You shall love the Lord your God with all your heart, and with all your soul, and with all your mind" (Matthew 22:37).

It is evident that the mind is an important faculty through which we love God. Our mind is not to be arrogantly used by a proud soul as that which is set over and above the Word, critiquing the Word, picking and choosing what we will believe. Rather, we are subject to the Word as we attempt to understand it. We are to engage in sanctified thought. This is something to consider: We are not only to love God with all our hearts, but with all of our minds as well. In the same fashion, we are not only to receive the love of God with our whole hearts, but our *minds* are also a means of receiving the love the Trinity has for us. Here is another instance of a holy conviction:

> Just as it is written, "For your sake we are being put to death all day long, we were considered as sheep to be slaughtered." But in all these things we overwhelmingly conquer through Him who loved us. For I am convinced that neither death, nor life, nor angels, nor principalities, nor things present, nor things to come, nor powers, nor height, nor depth, nor any other created thing, will be able to separate us from the love of God, which is in Christ Jesus our Lord (Romans 8:36–39).

Paul wrote, "I am convinced." Are you convinced? Paul was persuaded by Calvary, the evidence of God's love. He was convinced through the experience of receiving the outpouring of the Holy Spirit. We should press into knowing God's love subjectively and objectively. We should consider what we have experienced and believed and seek to understand life through what we have known. This will be a springboard into practical demonstrations of His love to others.

## Chapter Summary

Paul serves as an exceptional example for the body of Messiah. Not only did this Apostle personally embrace the love of God, but he also left us a record of how he related to this love. Paul taught us to receive and embrace the objective love of God, to believe what the cross is communicating. He also let us know that subjective experience of this love is the norm. In other words, he encouraged faith based upon evidence which will open the door for an experience of this love. He also interpreted and gave content to the subjective experience of God's love within the context of the objective revelation of the Scriptures, in particular, Calvary. Furthermore, with the words "how much more…" Paul set an example of sanctified thought when he drew faith-filled conclusions founded upon the testimony and experience of God's love. Paul's writings invite us to follow his example and press in to know this love, affirming it by faith, embracing the experience, thinking about the ramifications of this love, and allowing it to shape our perspective of the rest of life.

## Consider

> But God demonstrates His own love toward us, in that while we were yet sinners, Christ died for us (Romans 5:8).

The Demonstrator is the God of glory. He shines upon and enjoys the adoration of multitudes of angelic majesties. When these messengers are manifest to humanity they must often rebuke the worship which stunned prophets mistakenly proffer. These "glories" worship Him. This is the One Who, through love, opened Himself up to the full sense of humiliation.

Through the crucifixion, love's eternal light extinguished Himself. Through Jesus' death, God found a way to become "not." In the incarnation's culmination, the Almighty exerted effort past the point of exhaustion. Omnipotence expired in Messiah as He gave the last drop of life. Supreme labor! Majestic weakness! Infinite love poured out to fill a seemingly insatiable need – forgiveness for humanity; the reconciliation of the utterly alienated. God in Jesus manifested this.

So, how much does He love us? To what lengths is He willing to go to save us? How deep is His desire for us to return to Him? Is there a higher demonstration of love the Creator could give? Ask for empowering grace to grasp this love.

1.  What is the most important truth you learned in this chapter?

2.  List the three aspects to Paul's understanding of knowing the love of God.

3.  What is your favorite passage or verse upon which your faith rests concerning the love of God?

4.  Have you ever experienced the love of God in a subjective manner? If so, describe that experience. If not, are you open to such an experience, why or why not?

5.  Please read Philippians 4:8:

    > Finally, brethren, whatever is true, whatever is honorable, whatever is right, whatever is pure, whatever is lovely, whatever is of good repute, if there is any excellence and if anything worthy of praise, dwell on these things.

    How can sanctified thought help you to fulfill this verse?

6.  What did you struggle with the most in this chapter? Consider taking further time to study the Scriptures about this topic, and commit it to prayer.

7.  Please paraphrase, personalize and pray through Galatians 2:20b:

    > The life which I now live in the flesh I live by faith in the Son of God, who loved me and gave Himself up for me.

*The love of God is greater far*
*Than tongue or pen can ever tell;*
*It goes beyond the highest star,*
*And reaches to the lowest hell...*
*Could we with ink the ocean fill,*
*And were the skies of parchment made,*
*Were every stalk on earth a quill,*
*And every man a scribe by trade,*
*To write the love of God above,*
*Would drain the ocean dry.*
*Nor could the scroll contain the whole,*
*Though stretched from sky to sky.*

FREDERICK M. LEHMAN, MEIR BEN ISAAC NEHORAI

*Can you discover the depths of God?*
*Can you discover the limits of the Almighty?*
*They are high as the heavens, what can you do?*
*Deeper than Sheol, what can you know?*
*Its measure is longer than the earth*
*And broader than the sea.*

ZOPHAR THE NAAMATHITE, *Job 11:7–9*

*It is impossible to grasp the divine purpose in all its dimensions without knowing the love of Christ — and this cannot be other than an experimental knowledge.*

F. F. BRUCE, *The Epistles to the Colossians,*
*to Philemon, and to the Ephesians*

## Chapter 4

# Grasping the Love of God

*...may have power, together with all of the saints, to grasp how wide and long and high and deep is the love of Christ (Ephesians 3:18 NIV).*

WE'VE SPENT THE LAST THREE CHAPTERS laying a foundation for understanding how important the love of God is supposed to be in the life of a believer. Just to review: we've seen the love of God in Jesus' life, in His commandments, in John's life, in Peter's life, in Paul's life. We've seen the love of God becoming a foundation for the Apostles, being personalized, being thought about, and being passed along. If we want to form a New Testament perspective of the value of the love of God in the life of a believer we can definitively say: it is significant. Personalizing the love of God is supposed to be a real part of our relationship with God. The knowledge of the love of God is supposed to be an ongoing experience. We're commanded to deeply and personally receive His love. We are to know the objective evidence, and have faith in the Word. We are to be brought into the awareness of this love by the Spirit. The New Testament reveals a phenomenal role the love of God is to play in our walk with God.

### Ephesians 3: An Important Passage

Now that we've seen that we are supposed to live in an ongoing awareness of the love of God, we need to answer a relevant question: *how?* A great introductory answer is found in Ephesians 3, one of the most powerful and informative New Testament passages concerning the love of God.

In Ephesians 3 we get a glimpse into the prayer life of an Apostle. Often enough Paul tells the believers that he is praying for them; here he reveals some of the content of his prayers. If we believe that this man was inspired by the Spirit of God, then we should pay attention to how he prayed and to the theme of this Apostolic intercessor's petition. Such prayers reveal God's will.

In addition, this prayer is vital to us because it is enscriptured; we know that everything in Scripture is important, and everything in Scripture is inspired. This is a God-breathed, Apostle-prayed, significant passage. Let's give heed to what is going on here.

> For this reason I kneel before the Father, from whom His whole family in heaven and on earth derives its name. I pray that out of His glorious riches He may strengthen you with power through His Spirit in your inner being, so that Christ may dwell in your hearts through faith. And I pray that you, being rooted and established in love, may have power, together with all the saints, to grasp how wide and long and high and deep is the love of Christ, and to know this love that surpasses knowledge – that you may be filled to the measure of all the fullness of God. Now to Him who is able to do immeasurably more than all we ask or imagine, according to His power that is at work within us, to Him be glory in the church and in Christ Jesus throughout all generations, for ever and ever! Amen (Ephesians 3:14–21 NIV).

## Going Deeper

Now, let's examine some aspects of this passage.

**Verses 14–15. For this reason I bow my knees before the Father, from whom every family in heaven and on earth derives its name.**

This position of kneeling indicates desperation and intensity of desire. This was no casual prayer. This was earnest, fervent petition. Paul really wanted God to do something for the Ephesian believers, so much so that he took the position of begging. What was he so intently asking for?

**Verse 16. ...that He would grant you, according to the riches of His glory, to be strengthened with power through His Spirit in the inner man...**

Paul prayed that these people would have the subjective experience of receiving strength in their inner man through the agency of the Holy Spirit. To what end?

**Verse 17. ...so that Christ may dwell in your hearts through faith; and that you, being rooted and grounded in love...**

The first of Paul's objectives is that the Messiah would dwell in their hearts via faith. Secondly, that the Ephesians would be rooted and grounded in His love. We should recognize that as we are strengthened by the Spirit, we are enabled to receive an intensifying of the indwelling of Jesus and be planted in and founded upon His love.

Let's look at the content of this verse a little more deeply. To make his point, Paul uses two different metaphors. "Being rooted" speaks of the life of a plant and "grounded" refers to a building. Paul is particularly fond of this pattern. In his epistles he uses this combination of agricultural and architectural metaphors two other times. Here they are:

> ...having been firmly rooted and now being built up in Him and established in your faith, just as you were instructed, and overflowing with gratitude (Colossians 2:7).

> For we are God's fellow workers; you are God's field, God's building (1 Corinthians 3:9).

In Ephesians 3:17, Paul prayed that as a result of Messiah's indwelling we would be rooted in and founded upon Jesus' love. To what do these metaphors point?

## God Wants Us Rooted in the Love of Jesus

What does it mean to be rooted? Roots are the least attractive part of a tree. They are taken for granted and are generally not seen. Yet roots are a vital part of a plant's anatomy. Though unseen, they provide stability and nourishment. Without roots, a tree cannot stand. If the root system is weak, the tree will not be able to survive in difficult times. Without roots, a tree cannot thrive. In addition, roots grow. Roots are alive. They break through or overcome obstacles. One factor in the size of a plant is the amount of space the roots have to reach down and spread out. Another factor in the health of a plant is the quality of the soil in which it is rooted.

The soil of God's love contains the right nutrients for the plant of your life, relationships and calling. This soil allows the water of the Spirit to reach the deepest, most essential, far-reaching aspects of the roots of your life (Isaiah 44:3–4). God's love provides the roots of your life with the stability that can withstand the winds of circumstance. These roots grant balance and strength. By being rooted in the love of God, you will be able to receive all that is necessary for growth. Being rooted in this love is key to becoming fruitful. You are called to be thoroughly rooted in His love.

## God Wants Us Grounded in His Love

Again, a simple question, what does it mean to be grounded? Let's consider this word "grounded." The word has to do with being founded or established. It implies being built upon something, as a building is built upon its foundation. If properly constructed, buildings do not move from their foundations. The foundation determines the stability, height and size of the building. Every foundation is constructed with the purpose of supporting the vision of the architect: the shape, size, and function of the intended building.

God's love is the foundation, and we are being built, we are under construction on that foundation. Like a building, this foundation is the key to our stability, shape and size. How broad, long, high and deep is this foundation? What is the "breadth and length and height and depth" of this love? A key to understanding your immediate purpose and eternal destiny is seeing the extent of the foundation upon which you are being built. We have a big foundation. Its size is beyond knowing, we cannot plumb its depths. Our foundation is the love of Jesus. The builder and architect of our lives is God (Hebrews 11:10).

These two metaphors describe two aspects of knowing God's love. "Rooted" speaks of growth which is the result of living effort. Having strong roots is essential to your health and stability. The health and strength of your roots help determine the potential of your growth in God. Everyone has roots, but not everyone is rooted in the healthy soil of God's love.

"Grounded" speaks of the stability that comes from resting. Everyone is relying upon something, but not everyone is resting upon God's love.

Paul pleaded with the Father that the Ephesians would experience a victorious stability in the midst of spiritual conflict (Ephesians 6:10–20). They were to be immovable as a result of a determined spiritual pursuit, which implies progressive growth. They were also called to stand, experiencing the outcome of resting by faith upon that which is absolute. These activities were to take place at the same time.

While we are growing *into* the experiential knowledge of His love, we are also to be resolutely relying *upon* the objective reality of His love. The vastness of this love (soil) into which we are to grow and the enormity of the foundation upon which we are being built give hints as to God's eternal purposes:

> Beloved, now we are children of God, and it has not appeared as yet what we will be. We know that when He appears, we will be like Him, because we will see Him just as He is (1 John 3:2).

## The Key to Grasping

Let's continue to examine Paul's prayer in the next verse.

**Verse 18.   ...may have power, together with all the saints, to grasp how wide and long and high and deep is the love of Christ** (NIV).

As we noted in the last verse, the Spirit strengthens us so that the Messiah may dwell in us through faith and that we would be rooted and grounded in love. Paul goes on to pray for the outcome of this experience: the resultant release of power for the purpose of grasping the fullness of the dimensions of Jesus' love. The ability to grasp the love of God comes from God. That is why Paul is driven to prayer. He realizes that even divinely inspired instruction is not sufficient. Believers need to be empowered by God to grasp the love of God. In the final analysis, for Paul, our experiential knowledge of God's love is dependent upon God.

The Greek word for "power" is: *exischuo*. It carries this sense: to be totally, highly, completely skilled and therefore able to accomplish or experience something. It indicates overall adequacy and the full capacity – enough strength – to be completely capable to bring about the desired result – to be strong enough to fulfill what is required or desired. In this verse it is indicating a Spirit-given ability; it is an anointing.

The Greek word for "grasp" is *katalambano*, and it is intended to communicate intensity, immediateness, and certainty of possession in both the physical and intellectual arenas. *Katalambano* indicates coming to understand something which was not comprehended immediately prior to its being grasped.

The sense of the Greek word for "grasp" is similar to the English word "epiphany," which is a sudden comprehension, like a moment of "enlightenment," when something suddenly makes sense to you or becomes perfectly clear. That is "grasping." Through His Spirit, the Father can grant you a sudden and clear revelation of this love which is past finding out.

In reality, this Spirit-enabled revelation is necessary for our hearts; we are *dependent* upon the anointing of God to experience this power to grasp. Without grasping we cannot abide, because the ability to grasp the love of God *precedes* the ability to abide in His love. If you can't take hold of it, you are not going to be able to stay there. Therefore, in order to abide in the love of God, we need an anointing to supernaturally grasp His love. This comes through the Holy Spirit, from God Himself, in answer to prayer. The power to grasp is available.

**Verse 19.  …and to know the love of Christ which surpasses knowledge, that you may be filled up to all the fullness of God.**

We only have time to briefly mention this here, but it is important to know: Grasping this love has significant benefits in the life of the believer: Fullness is pretty significant! What is this fullness like? Jesus is the image and fullness of God (Colossians 1:15, 2:9). Jesus' life on earth demonstrated what the fullness of God looks like. What will the believer being filled with the fullness of God look like? In our lives, fullness will look like Jesus.

In Ephesians 1:23 Paul reveals that the Church is the fullness of Him Who fills all in all. Now, in the passage we're focusing on, it is as if Paul says: "Here's the key to experiencing what you are. You're to know the love of the Messiah which surpasses knowledge so you will be filled with all the fullness of God."

This thought is foreign to us. We may contend, "That's not how you get to be filled with all of the fullness of God. You've got to fast for it."

"No," another says, "sell all you have and give it to the poor. That's how to get filled."

Yet another, "Take upon yourself the role of a servant; there are toilets that need to be scrubbed. That's how you get filled with all of the fullness of God."

All of these disciplines and principles are good and may be necessary. Yet, how did Paul write it? What did the Holy Spirit reveal? How did Paul pray for this glorious goal?

> I pray that you, being rooted and established in love, may have power...to grasp...and to know this love...that you may be filled to the measure of all the fullness of God (Ephesians 3:17–19 NIV).

As we grasp, we are increasingly being filled with an ultimate result: grasping God's love leads to looking like Jesus. We will be conformed to Jesus' inner reality, the experience of His Father's love. We are promised that we will be filled with a fullness internally that resembles Messiah externally. This is a phenomenal reality! Though our instinctual response may reflexively say that we can never resemble Jesus to such a tremendous extent, look at these verses:

> ...and to know the love of Christ which surpasses knowledge, that you may be filled up to all the fullness of God. Now to Him who is able to do far more abundantly beyond all that we ask or think, according to the power that works within us, to Him be the glory in the church and in Christ Jesus to all generations forever and ever. Amen (Ephesians 3:19–21).

This doxology provides us with the cause of our confidence in the outcome of this loving relational process. The Almighty is able to accomplish His aim of conforming us to the pattern of the Messiah. He is aggressively determined to achieve the apparently impossible and do way more than we dare to desire or imagine. The power that is at work in us is the miraculous might Father imparted to us by His Spirit. No wonder Paul prophetically calls for praise and honor to be eternally offered to God. What a goal! What a process! What a wonderful God!

## Review

Paul's prayer in Ephesians 3 is a petition for an outpouring of the Holy Spirit upon the inner man, that as a result of His active presence there will be an increase of the dynamic of strength (by the Spirit) in their innermost beings. This is a prayer for the increase of enabling grace-to-grasp more than the Ephesians were already experiencing of Jesus' life within their hearts. This prayer gives us the "way" to grasp: God will give us an anointing of the Holy Spirit that enables us. Paul stresses the outcome of this experiential knowledge of the Lord Jesus' love. He wrote that the results of grasping and knowing this love will be this: the believers will be filled up to "all the fullness of God."

## The Necessity of the Spirit's Involvement

Now that we've seen that abiding comes through grasping and grasping comes through the Spirit's help, let's consider the Holy Spirit's involvement in our receiving the love of God.

From the beginning to the end of Jesus' life, we see the Spirit's important enabling activity; the Holy Spirit enabled Messiah to accomplish what He set out to do – the will of His Father. At the climax of Jesus' ministry and obedience, the Spirit enabled the Messiah to offer Himself up to God (Hebrews 9:14). If this is how the

Spirit interacted with Jesus, it shouldn't surprise us that the Spirit is absolutely necessary for our own life in God. So, how does the knowledge of our need translate into a capacity to comprehend this love? How does the awareness of our need for the anointing affect our own apprehension of the love of God?

Let's revisit Jesus' directive to abide in His love. When this command was given, Jesus was about to accomplish His Passion. He was looking forward to His Ascension and Enthronement. He would no longer physically be with the disciples. Yet, He commanded them to abide in His love. How could this be possible? Jesus said:

> I will ask the Father, and He will give you another Helper, that He may be with you forever; that is the Spirit of truth, whom the world cannot receive, because it does not see Him or know Him, but you know Him because He abides with you and will be in you. I will not leave you as orphans; I will come to you (John 14:16–18).

Messiah said He would not leave them bereft, but He would be present through the presence of the Spirit of Truth. Through this Spirit the Apostles would be able to abide in Jesus' present love.

Similarly, Paul directed the believers' attention to the dynamic presence of the Spirit. The Spirit conveyed God's love to their hearts.

> And hope does not disappoint, because the love of God has been poured out within our hearts through the Holy Spirit who was given to us (Romans 5:5).

Like Jesus, we experience God's love through Abba's presence and activity by His Spirit. Like Jesus, we are called to live in the experience of God's love "by the love of the Spirit..." (Romans 15:30b). We cannot overestimate the crucial nature of the Holy Spirit's role. He strengthens our innermost being that Jesus may dwell there by faith; He conveys the love of God.

If we're to abide in His love, it is not going to be done because we have good minds, have made a decision to do it, or are diligent to study this truth. Rather, the Holy Spirit will enable us to grasp God's love.

This should be an encouragement to us. Abba will accomplish this in us as we turn to Him; we don't have to "figure out" the love of God for ourselves. The Holy Spirit will give us the power to grasp this love. Let's turn to Father, Who gives us His Spirit, and ask Him to pour out His Spirit upon us so we may be empowered to grasp.

> If you then, being evil, know how to give good gifts to your children, how much more will your heavenly Father give the Holy Spirit to those who ask Him? (Luke 11:13)

Since the knowledge of this love is a necessity, we should make the attaining of it a priority. Some are concerned that if we ask God for further experience with the Holy Spirit we may end up in fanaticism or deception. To emphasize the importance of asking God for His Spirit, let's view Luke 11:13 in its context:

> So I say to you, ask, and it will be given to you; seek, and you will find; knock, and it will be opened to you. For everyone who asks, receives; and he who seeks, finds; and to him who knocks, it will be opened. Now suppose one of you fathers is asked by his son for a fish; he will not give him a snake instead of a fish, will he? Or if he is asked for an egg, he will not give him a scorpion, will he? If you then, being evil, know how to give good gifts to your children, how much more will your heavenly Father give the Holy Spirit to those who ask Him? (Luke 11:9–13)

Our teacher and example, Jesus, encourages us to confidently, consistently, persistently pursue the promise of our good Father to give us His Spirit. Only through the Holy Spirit are we able to have the power to grasp the knowledge of Jesus' love. It is absolutely necessary for the Holy Spirit to gift us with that power, for this love is far too vast for our comprehension. In Ephesians 3, Paul recognizes this, and prays. And what is Paul's prayer?

> For this reason I bow my knees before the Father...that He would grant you, according to the riches of His glory, to be strengthened with power through His Spirit in the inner man, so that Christ may dwell in your hearts through faith; and that you, being rooted and grounded in love, may be able to comprehend with all the saints what is the breadth and length and height and depth, and to know the love of Christ which surpasses knowledge, that you may be filled up to all the fullness of God (Ephesians 3:14, 16–19).

Notice how Paul begins with a petition for an outpouring of the Holy Spirit to empower believers. The purpose of that empowerment is twofold, so that "Christ may dwell in your heart" and "that you...may be able to comprehend" the Messiah's love. We need the Holy Spirit to give us the ability to grasp how much Jesus loves us. Let's join our hearts to the Scriptures and pray that He would make this love (which surpasses knowledge) known through the Spirit's anointing to grasp.

## Consider

Your life is supposed to be established upon the love of Jesus. How broad, long, high and deep is this foundation? What is the "breadth and length and height and depth" of this love?

A key to understanding your eternal destiny is seeing the extent of the foundation upon which you are being built. This is a big foundation. It is past finding out. It is the love of Jesus.

There is nothing lacking in the foundation, but our faith-understanding of how reliable this love is can grow. The greater your faith-understanding of the love of God, the freer to know, follow and express God you'll be.

You can be built upon this foundation; you can increase in your knowledge of, and confidence in, His love. Spend time considering the "breadth and length and height and depth of the love of God."

1. What is the most important truth you learned in this chapter?

2. "Without grasping, we can not abide...If you can't take hold of it, you are not going to be able to stay there." This statement is a pattern for other areas of spiritual truth. Have you experienced grasping and subsequent abiding in any area of your spiritual life? Describe this experience.

3. The overall pattern of the Ephesians 3 passage is this: Prayer leads to the activity of the Spirit, which leads to grasping, which leads to being filled. Have you come to believe that God can enable you to grasp His love as you seek Him for this experience? Why, or why not?

4. Have you sought to know the love, approval, and affection of God through means other than Spirit-enabled grasping? Examples might be: through study, through careful obedience.

5. Please read 1 John 2:27:

   > As for you, the anointing which you received from Him abides in you, and you have no need for anyone to teach you; but as His anointing teaches you about all things, and is true and is not a lie, and just as it has taught you, you abide in Him.

   What does it mean that the Spirit teaches us to abide? How will this impact your own efforts to grasp the love of God?

*By knowing the love of Christ, and only so, is it possible to be filled up to the measure of God's own fullness. This, one may say, is the language of hyperbole: how can the finite reach the infinite? But the Christ whose love is to be known is the Christ in whom "all the fullness of deity resides" and in whom his people have found their fullness (Colossians 2:9–10). By the knowledge of his love, and only so, may they hope to attain to the divine fullness – insofar as that attainment is possible for created beings.*

F. F. BRUCE, *The Epistle to the Colossians, to Philemon, and to the Ephesians*

*We sometimes fear to bring our troubles to God, because they must seem small to Him who sitteth on the circle of the earth. But if they are large enough to vex and endanger our welfare, they are large enough to touch His heart of love.*

R. A. TORREY

*No cord nor cable can so forcibly draw, or hold so fast, as love can do with a twined thread.*

ROBERT BURTON

*First, it is essential that you understand God's posture towards you…He wants to fellowship with you forever.*

MICHAEL L. BROWN

# Chapter 5

# The Promised Outcome

*...and to know the love of Christ which surpasses knowledge, that you may be filled up to all the fullness of God (Ephesians 3:19).*

THE CHOICE TO PURSUE the knowledge of the love of God is going to produce practical and spiritual results in our lives. Let's look at the fruit this will produce. We'll begin by returning to Ephesians 3:19 to further explore the concept of the "fullness of God." Before we start examining specific benefits of knowing God's love, we need to see what the ultimate goal looks like.

## "Fullness" in Ephesians

In the letter to the Ephesians, the word "fullness" is introduced in Ephesians 1:10 and echoed in 1:23, 3:19, and 4:13. We're going to look briefly at three of these verses so we can see the theme of "fullness" as mentioned in Ephesians 3:19 in some of its context. We will return to 3:19 a bit later. Let's begin with Ephesians 1:10:

> ...with a view to an administration suitable to the fullness of the times, that is, the summing up of all things in Christ, things in the heavens and things on the earth. In Him...

This verse speaks of fullness in terms of time. "The fullness of the times" refers to completion, to fulfillment, to the accomplished purposes of God. It has to do with the whole cosmos being summed up in Messiah: the ultimate fulfillment of God's redemptive plans. That epoch is referred to by Paul as the fullness of times.

> And He put all things in subjection under His feet, and gave Him as head over all things to the church, which is His body, the fullness of Him who fills all in all (Ephesians 1:22–23).

We see later in the same chapter that the Church contains the fullness of Jesus' life and is the focal point of the Messiah's redemptive activity. The Church fulfills the role of releasing Jesus' manifest presence and dynamic activity in the world.

> And He gave some as apostles, and some as prophets, and some as evangelists, and some as pastors and teachers, for the equipping of the saints for the work of service, to the building up of the body of Christ; until we all attain to the unity of the faith, and of the knowledge of the Son of God, to a mature man, to the measure of the stature which belongs to the fullness of Christ (Ephesians 4:11–13).

Ephesians 4:13: "…to the fullness of Christ." The Ascension Gifts will minister in the Body until the Second Coming. The fruition of God's labor will see the full measure of Jesus' life revealed in the redeemed. "Fullness" proceeds from and belongs to Messiah Jesus. True ministry ultimately will release His fullness in the body of Messiah. The fullness of the Messiah is God in action in His people through the agency of the Holy Spirit. The very word used for "spirit" in Hebrew and Greek implies motion. *Ruach* or *pneuma* is not translated "air" but breath, wind, spirit. The fullness of Jesus in the Church will look like people who have been "born of the Spirit." They are like the wind – moved by the hand of God, doing the acts of God, not bound to merely earthly considerations.

Now let's focus on our text:

> …and to know the love of Christ which surpasses knowledge, that you may be filled up to all the fullness of God (Ephesians 3:19).

In concluding this divinely breathed intercession, we find Paul had a goal in mind – the Church being filled with all God is. We're beginning to discuss the benefits which proceed from knowing Jesus' love. The key to understanding these blessings is looking at what the term "the fullness of God" implies. Let's trace this process and describe this "fullness."

Let's ask Paul, "How can we receive the fullness of God?" In this section of Scripture, Paul hands the Church a revelatory key. He answers, "The key to experiencing fullness is knowing Messiah's love." There is an unanticipated consequence to knowing the love of God. The unlikely upshot of knowing Jesus' love is that the Church will "be filled up to all the fullness of God!"

Now, many sincere believers seek to attain fullness. Yet, the text says fullness is not achieved, rather (like "salvation") it is received. In this case, it is received through Paul's intercession and the Father's resultant activity. The process here is this: fullness comes from Father, through Jesus, by the Holy Spirit, in answer to prayer. It is the result of knowing the full dimensions of Messiah's love.

That fullness is "received" cannot be more clearly stated than in this passage. In fact, this is the essential passage in the New Testament that speaks to the issue of experiencing the fullness of God. According to Paul's prayer, knowing the Messiah's love is the key to fullness. Paul prayed for the believers to experience this love to the end that they "may be filled up to all the fullness of God." Every other help towards the immediate and eschatological expression of fullness is supplementary to this holy process which, amazingly, is also the end itself – the knowledge of God and His love.

Jesus is the perfect picture of the fullness of God. Look at these two verses:

> For it was the Father's good pleasure for all the fullness to dwell in Him (Colossians 1:19).

> For in Him all the fullness of Deity dwells in bodily form
> (Colossians 2:9).

Jesus is the pattern of what fullness looks like. As the Body grasps God's love, it participates in the process of being filled with God's fullness. When the Body is "filled up to all the fullness of God" it will resemble the Son of God. Again, how do we get filled up with all of the fullness of God? Paul points us in this direction, *"through knowing the love of Messiah."* What a wonderful plan God has!

> Things which eye has not seen and ear has not heard, and which
> have not entered the heart of man, all that God has prepared for
> those who love Him (1 Corinthians 2:9b).

We have already seen that pursuing a knowledge of the love of God will ultimately lead to the release of the fullness of God in our lives (Ephesians 3:19), causing our lives to look like Jesus, Who is the fullness of God in bodily form (Colossians 2:9).

So what does this fullness look like in our day-to-day lives? What is the practical fruit of a sustained relationship with God based upon experiencing Messiah's love? Let's consider some aspects of this fullness.

## Knowing God

Knowing God is one of the first vital benefits of knowing the love of God. In knowing God's love we get to know God, Himself. We can definitively assert that no one knew the Father like Jesus did:

> Nor does anyone know the Father except the Son, and anyone to
> whom the Son wills to reveal Him (Matthew 11:27b).

Jesus' knowledge of the Father was so intimate that the Father did nothing without sharing it with the Son:

> For the Father loves the Son, and shows Him all things that He Him-
> self is doing (John 5:20).

He also committed "all things" into Jesus' hands (John 3:35).

From this testimony we can deduce that Jesus' knowledge of the Father was accurate and complete. Our outlook is often off. His was never wrong. He did not have a skewed view of the Father. We see in part. He did not. His perception of the Father was not mediated through sin or the bitter wounds of life. Jesus really knew the Father.

As we enter in to our relationship with God through the doorway of abiding in His love, our intimacy will deepen. As we relate to Him on His terms ("abide in My love"), we will increasingly know Him as *He* desires to be known.

Abiding in God through Jesus brings us into conscious contact with His character. We know of His character from Scripture; He is good, faithful, zealous and kind. These virtues are wonderful and important, but the Lord also has a personality. Every believer should be convinced that, since Jesus is a person, He has a personality. But have we encountered it, or do we merely "take it by faith"? As you get to know the love of God you will come into contact with His personality.

Not only does God have a character and a personality, but He has plans. If you spend sufficient time with anybody, you get to know their character, their personality, and their dreams, desires, and plans. You get to know their immediate focus and become familiar with their long-term goals. This is true of God as well; as you abide in the love of the Messiah, you will get to know His plans, intentions, and goals better.

Taking this aspect of knowing God into consideration, you can look at it as if He promised: "If you spend time with Me, you're going to know My character, My personality, and you're going to know My dreams, desires, and plans. You'll get to know what I'm focused on, where My attention is. You're going to know Me a whole lot better." Do you want to experience Jesus' character, personality, and plans? *"Abide in Me; abide in My love."*

Knowing God is an important aspect of the fullness which Jesus models.

## A Secure Relationship

Not only will you know God better through grasping His love, but knowing God's love transforms your relationship with Him and places your relationship with Him on firm ground (Ephesians 3:17). We will have more security and stability in God when we abide in His love.

When you are saturated with the Messiah's love you will rely on Him with greater assurance. Look at how boldly Jesus prayed at Lazarus' tomb:

> So they removed the stone. Then Jesus raised His eyes, and said, "Father, I thank You that You have heard Me. I knew that You always hear Me; but because of the people standing around I said it, so that they may believe that You sent Me." When He had said these things, He cried out with a loud voice, "Lazarus, come forth" (John 11:41–43).

When you know that an exceptional person is lovingly committed to you, you can boldly rely upon him.

> For by You I can run upon a troop; by my God I can leap over a wall (2 Samuel 22:30).

> If God is for us, who is against us? (Romans 8:31b).

## Obedient Trust

Inevitably, this boldness will overflow into faith-filled obedience. Knowing the love of your God will give you increased confidence and faith in His intentions and purposes in your life. You will be able to obey more freely, entrusting yourself more completely to His loving care.

Jesus "endured the cross, despising the shame" because of His confidence that the Father would assuredly fulfill the promise of the "joy set before Him" (Hebrews 12:2). It is an amazing reality that Jesus was convinced of the joy waiting for Him on the other side of the cross. At times we pass through minor trials and lose all sight of God's goodness and care. Yet Jesus, facing the ultimate trial – total separation from God – was able to maintain an expectancy of **joy.** This is extreme faith, faith that does not waver in the face of death. This faith will be ours in increasing measure as we embrace Messiah's love for us.

## A Grateful Response

Another longed for and needed benefit is this: Truly knowing the love of God will produce a reciprocal response. When you are receiving a wonderful love, you will respond in kind, seeking to love, bless, and serve the beloved.

> We love, because He first loved us (1 John 4:19).

Jesus gave the testimony: "For I always do the things that are pleasing to Him" (John 8:29b). We see Jesus seeking to please Father with all of His heart, soul, mind, and strength. Likewise, when you know the fullness of Jesus' love you will respond commensurately. You will love because He first loved you. His love elicits gratitude. His fiery love sparks a similar response. What many cannot attain through determination and sheer willpower comes easily as our hearts yearn to respond to His incredible love.

## Sanctification

Part of the fullness of God in the Body, modeled by the Son of God, is consecrated devotion to God, Himself. Knowing this love will release a complete orientation towards God. This orientation will produce a consequent holiness of motivation and action: an intensity of devotion that would embarrass most of our experiences that we call "first love." This love-based relationship will bring about consecration to the King and His purposes. An example of this consecration in mature fruition can be found at Gethsemane.

> And He went a little beyond them, and fell on His face and prayed, saying, "My Father, if it is possible, let this cup pass from Me; yet not as I will, but as You will" (Matthew 26:39).

This is perhaps the ultimate example of consecration in the Scriptures: Jesus, choosing His Father's will over His own, even unto death. Has God's love captured your heart? Are you responding to His initiation? Does the desire to reciprocate stir your soul?

## Freedom to Relate

A further benefit of abiding in the love of God is the recovery of true liberty in our relationship with God. This is not liberty to do whatever you want, to sin in whatever way catches your fancy. In fact, if you've been born again, those very thoughts would be alien to you. They would bring about a *"may-it-never-be!"* from the depths of your soul.

> What shall we say then? Are we to continue in sin so that grace may increase? May it never be! How shall we who died to sin still live in it? (Romans 6:1–2).

> What then? Shall we sin because we are not under law but under grace? May it never be! (Romans 6:15).

So what is our liberty? The greatest freedom found through the experience of God's love is confidence to communicate freely with Him.

> Therefore let us draw near with confidence to the throne of grace, so that we may receive mercy and find grace to help in time of need (Hebrews 4:16).

We come before Him and communicate with boldness. The word *confidence* here means complete freedom of speech. That, by the way, does not mean a temper tantrum; we must maintain reverence for God. This liberty is not license to say whatever we may want, however we may want to say it. Yet, in that which is vital we are not bound by concerns like, "Is it appropriate if I say this or not?"

Look again at Jesus in the garden of Gethsemane. Three times He prayed: "Let this cup pass from Me." This is self disclosure. This is the Son of God unburdening His heart. This is honesty about the Messiah's antipathy to the shame and agony of what was to come. Jesus was confident enough in the Father's love to candidly share His struggle. The Father wants us to communicate openly and honestly with Him. Through knowing the love of God, we will recover true liberty in our communication with God.

## Hearing His Voice

Along with open reverent communication comes complete confidence in God's ability to speak with you, accompanying a bedrock assurance that He wants to. God is not only able to speak with you, but to communicate with you is His earnest desire. You can be assured that God does – and will – speak with you. Knowing the Messiah's love increases our confidence in God's willingness and desire to communicate with us. Faith is an important key to opening the door to hearing God. As you're convinced of God's love, you'll believe He wants to communicate with you. Why? Because He loves you. Love seeks to communicate. Here is the pattern: "For the Father loves the Son, and shows Him all things that He Himself is doing" (John 5:20). When you know the overflow of Jesus' love you will have more freedom in communicating your heart to God, and in hearing Him more often, more easily!

My sheep hear My voice, and I know them, and they follow Me (John 10:27; see also John 10:3–5,8,16).

But when He, the Spirit of truth, comes, He will guide you into all the truth; for He will not speak on His own initiative, but whatever He hears, He will speak; and He will disclose to you what is to come. He will glorify Me, for He will take of Mine and will disclose it to you (John 16:13–14).

## Worship

The knowledge of the love of God is also the cornerstone of thanksgiving and praise.

I have trusted in Your lovingkindness; my heart shall rejoice in Your salvation (Psalm 13:5).

Certainly, God's love is the fountain of thanksgiving in the midst of difficult circumstances.

The LORD is my strength and my shield; my heart trusts in Him, and I am helped; therefore my heart exults, and with my song I shall thank Him (Psalm 28:7).

Yet, joyous praise is not simply centered on what He has done, but on Who He is and why He's done it. Knowing His love is like entering the Holy of Holies. You will not only know His acts but also His ways.

Take My yoke upon you and learn from Me, for I am gentle and humble in heart, and you will find rest for your souls (Matthew 11:29).

The LORD is good to all, and His mercies are over all His works (Psalm 145:9).

Get to know the extravagance of Messiah's love for you and you will worship more intimately, give thanks more deeply, and praise Him joyously.

## Chapter Summary

We could go on and on with this list of the benefits of knowing the love of God. It affects every area of our lives. Paul summed it up for us as being "filled with all of the fullness of God." Jesus is the fullness of God; He is our model. The fullness of God in our lives will cause us to look like Jesus. Our relationship with the Father will look like Jesus' relationship with the Father.

As we discover how much God loves us we will increase in reliance upon God. Our devotion and consecration to Him and His purposes will be strengthened. We will be enabled to embrace a lifestyle of faith-filled obedience. We will recover liberty in communication with the Father, both in sharing our heart with Him, and in hearing His voice. We will have a heart response of willingly offering ourselves to Him as He has offered Himself to us. Our hearts will be filled with worship, adoration, and gratitude. Our lives will be transformed by knowing this love, transformed into the image of Jesus.

## Consider

As you increasingly come to believe God loves you, you will increasingly experience His love. More of life is rightly comprehended when we are truly apprehended by God's love. Why? Because faith opens the door.

Apart from faith it is impossible for us to please God (Hebrews 11:6a). We are called to walk by faith. How can we expect this type of faith (born out of relationship) to exist without knowing God's love?

If we don't believe He loves us, we are going to continually misconstrue the meaning of our lives, employing another interpretation. We will perceive something other than His love; our insight will be erroneous.

If we believe He loves us, we will be able to see Him setting up, or redeeming, circumstances around us with a loving motive. We will be able to embrace the heart of God's purposes for us with confidence. We will *not* be frightened of the objectives of God for our lives.

This doesn't mean that there is not an enemy or that we will not experience hardship in this life. It just means that even in the midst of warfare or intense trial, God is with us. **"This I know,"** the Psalmist said, **"that God is for me"** (Psalm 56:9b). Do we *know* that?

1.    What is the most important truth you learned in this chapter?

2.    Reread Ephesians 3:19. Have you ever desired to be filled with the fullness of God? Have you ever recognized that knowing the love of God is the key to being filled with God's fullness? What have you looked to as a key to fullness in your life? Is there Scriptural support for pursuing fullness in these ways?

3.    A child who is secure in his or her parents' love would most likely be more self-confident in life. Can you list some other benefits of being loved?

4.    Do you see areas in your life where there is lack because you have not experienced being loved? Do you believe an experiential awareness of God's love for you can change these areas?

5.    The aspects of fullness which we have listed here are far from complete. Considering the life of Jesus, can you think of other aspects of fullness that knowing His love might produce in your life?

6.    What did you struggle with the most in this chapter? Consider taking further time to study the Scriptures about this topic, and commit it to prayer.

7.    Please paraphrase, personalize and pray through Ephesians 3:18–21:

> ...may be able to comprehend with all the saints what is the breadth and length and height and depth, and to know the love

of Christ which surpasses knowledge, that you may be filled up to all the fullness of God. Now to Him who is able to do far more abundantly beyond all that we ask or think, according to the power that works within us, to Him be the glory in the church and in Christ Jesus to all generations forever and ever. Amen.

# PART 2:

## *AGAPE*

*"…Agape…"*                                            THE SEPTUAGINT

*Classical theism's root metaphor of motion with God as the nonrelating pillar around which we move…affects the Christian understanding of divine love since it is seen as a one-way, purely active benevolence with no receptivity or passion.*

                                                       JOHN SANDERS

*In aweful and surprising truth, we are the objects of His love. You asked for a loving God: you have one. The great spirit you so lightly invoked, the "lord of terrible aspect," is present: not a senile benevolence that drowsily wishes you to be happy in your own way, not the cold philanthropy of a conscientious magistrate, not the care of a host who feels responsible for the comforts of his guests, but the consuming fire Himself, the Love that made the worlds, persistent as the artist's love for his work and despotic as a man's love for a dog, provident and venerable as a father's love for a child, jealous, inexorable, exacting as love between the sexes…It is certainly a burden of glory not only beyond our deserts but also, except in rare moments of grace, beyond our desiring.*

                                                       C. S. LEWIS

*Contrary to some popular teachings, love is an emotion.*

                                       RICK JOYNER, *The World Aflame*

Agapao: *to treat with affection, to caress, love, be fond of, Pass. to be beloved, 2. in N.T. to regard with brotherly love, II. of things, to be well pleased or contented at or with a thing, to be well pleased that…*

                                       *Liddell-Scott Lexicon*

## Chapter 6

# A New Perspective

*We have come to know and have believed the love which*
*God has for us. God is love and the one who abides in love*
*abides in God, and God abides in him (1 John 4:16).*

WHAT IS THE NATURE of the love God has for us? What is His love for humanity like? In the New Testament the primary word used to convey God's love is *agape*. To more fully grasp God's love we should seek to define this word. Many of you who are reading this book believe you already know exactly what *agape* means. Please take the time and carefully consider the next two chapters. You may be pleasantly surprised.

The Greek word *agape*, which is simply translated "love" in the New Testament, is a subject much considered in our day. Teachings abound. Pastors, scholars, devotional writers, even secular sources have something to say about *agape*. Type *agape* into an online search engine and you will be amazed by what you find. In 2006 a trusted co-worker tried this, and the search engine pulled up over eight million "hits" that mention *agape*. That's a lot of "talk" about *agape*.

What are many of these people saying? Let's see if we can break this talk about *agape* down into a few manageable characteristics. Any one author or scholar might combine all of these things, but we're going to break them down to make it easier to understand.

## The God Type of Love

*Agape* is often called the "God-type" of love. Many say it is the highest type of love. In this understanding, this love is pure and perfect and not at all like our love. Here are two quotes that highlight this understanding of *agape*:

> "*Agape*, in the sense of Godlike love, is clearly distinguished from the rest. The first three are all natural, even to fallen man, whereas Godlike *agape*-love is not." *New Dictionary of Theology*

> "Love among persons is awakened by something in the beloved, but the love of God is free, spontaneous, unevoked, uncaused. God loves people because he has chosen to love them…and no reason for his love can be given except his own sovereign good pleasure." J. I. PACKER, *Knowing God*

These individuals might emphasize the death of Jesus in their understanding of *agape*; therefore *agape* would be manifest as perfectly selfless sacrificial action. As you can see, fallen man can hardly measure up to this definition of *agape*.

There are two primary ways people are taught to view *agape*. We'll call one "volitional love" and the other "unconditional love."

In the first understanding of *agape*, love is an act of the will; a determination to act lovingly. This would mean choosing to love someone even when you don't "feel like it." In other words, you don't really have any affection or other emotions associated with love – but you still choose to treat the person as if you loved them. In this view of *agape*, love is not emotional at all; rather it is Holy Morality (choosing to do what is right). Some say God's *agape* is volitional, meaning God chooses to love us, even though we are sinful and repulsive to God. In this view, God is the perfect moral Being. He always does what is right; therefore He acts like He "loves" us.

When people say *agape* is unconditional love, they are seeking to express the view that *agape* springs from God's loving nature. He *is* love, therefore He *does* love. Conversely they might say, "God loves because God is love." Because it is based in His nature there are no conditions to being loved (you don't earn it). And this love is given apart from any merit in any way (you also don't deserve it). Later in this book we will see that every condition for God's love has already been met.

## The Common Denominator

In the above views, God's love essentially has nothing to do with the objects of His love (meaning *us*)!

Let's look at how some authors describe this. Contained is a godly and effective popular writer, three theologians and an influential medieval mystic:

> "God loves you because He has chosen to do so." MAX LUCADO

> "Agape is sovereign in relation to its object, and is directed to both 'the evil and the good;' it is spontaneous, 'overflowing,' 'unmotivated.' " ANDERS NYGREN, *Agape and Eros*

> "Based neither on a felt need in the loving person nor on a desire called forth by some attractive feature(s) in the one loved..." *New Dictionary of Theology*

> "It is not a love of the worthy, and it is not a love that desires to possess." LEON MORRIS

> "The love with which we love should be so pure, so simple, so detached that it inclines neither to myself nor to my friend nor to anything else next to it." MEISTER ECKHARDT

In all of these explanations, *agape* is unattached, disinterested, unemotional towards us, gains nothing from us, wants nothing from us. In fact, this love bears no resemblance to what we know as love or "being loved" for it has no basis in desire, pleasure, or affection. It is devoid of many of the things we associate with love. We call this "the common understanding" of *agape*.

If we condense the common understanding of *agape* into a simple, clear definition, we could not do any better than the excellent explanation the *New Spirit Filled Life Bible* has provided. The following are the two definitions which are provided for *agape* as a verb and as a noun:

> (John 3:16) loved, agapao (ag-ah-pah-oh); Strong's #25: Unconditional love, love by choice and by act of the will. The word denotes unconquerable benevolence and undefeatable goodwill. Agapao will never seek anything but the highest good for fellow mankind. Agapao (the verb) and agape (the noun) are the words for God's unconditional love. It does not need a chemistry, an affinity, or a feeling. Agapao is a word that exclusively belongs to the Christian community. It is a love virtually unknown to writers outside the NT.

> (Romans 5:5) love, agape (ag-ah-pay); Strong's #26: A word to which Christianity gave new meaning. Outside of the NT, it rarely occurs in existing Greek manuscripts of the period. Agape denotes an undefeatable benevolence and unconquerable goodwill that always seeks the highest good of the other person, no matter what he does. It is the self-giving love that gives freely without asking anything in return, and does not consider the worth of its object. Agape is more a love by choice than philos, which is a love by chance; and it refers to the will rather than the emotion. Agape describes the unconditional love God has for the world.

## Reasons for Defining *Agape* This Way

Having now defined the common understanding of *agape*, we're going to scrutinize it in the light of Scripture, but first, let's consider some reasons people might define *agape* this way. We can't cover this extensively, but let's look at some of the more likely reasons people would define *agape* according to the common understanding.

## Theological Presuppositions

One possible cause for the nearly universal acceptance of the common understanding of *agape* might be that, today, *agape* is generally defined in conformity to a theological system and not according to its usage in the Bible. Some might reason that God is perfect — therefore He cannot desire us, really love us, long for us, feel remorse, etc. This could be linked to a fear of denigrating the majesty of God. People sincerely desire to avoid projecting human characteristics onto God. They want to maintain His perfection, His holiness, His absolute "otherness" in the way they understand perfection and holiness. In being extra careful not to belittle God, they define *agape* in a way that is far, far removed from all we commonly associate with love.

## Familiarity

The common understanding of *agape* is, in fact, the *common* understanding. As such, it is "taken for granted." There is a lot of writing and teaching out there. Sometimes, when something is ubiquitously and transgenerationally taught, we forget to carefully compare it to the Word of God. When there are currently eight million references to *agape* on the web, why would we feel a need to carefully examine the Scriptures to understand this one word? In this instance we have presumed that *agape* has been thoroughly studied. But does the common understanding of *agape* really line up with what we find in the Scriptures?

## Non-Hebraic Mindset

Many scholars and Bible teachers have not given appropriate consideration to the Hebraic background of the New Testament. The authors of the New Testament were Jewish believers in Yeshua (Jesus). As we noted when considering Peter, these men were steeped in the Hebrew Scriptures and the history and culture of their people. They were raised in Jewish homes. When they followed Jesus they did not stop observing the Jewish holy days or attending Jewish synagogues. Jesus is the *Jewish* Messiah. He fulfilled explicit and implicit prophetic expectations recorded in the Hebrew Scriptures. *Agape is* a Greek word, but it is a Greek word which is employed to translate a Hebrew concept.

## Agape, Ahavah, and the Septuagint

This theological blind spot is often revealed in the way scholars have interacted with the Hebrew word most commonly translated *love*: *ahavah*. According to the common consensus, *ahavah* is too general a term to accurately describe the love God displayed and Jesus commanded. They believe that, in contrast to *ahavah*, which is used to denote all kinds of love, the New Testament uses *agape* as a specific word which describes a love that is unique and divine. Indeed, I have heard it taught that *agape* was a rarely used word in Classical culture. I have read that the word *agape* was chosen by the New Testament writers precisely *because* of its seldom use. I've been told that, because of the unfamiliarity of this word, the inspired authors were able to redefine *agape* and invest in it a whole new supernatural meaning. It is widely celebrated as if it were a fact that this word, *agape*, is unique to Christianity and refers to a love which was never known before Jesus came.

Yet, there is much to contradict this view. This became clear to me when I studied every instance that *agape* is used in the New Testament. I then compared this with the way *ahavah* is used in the Hebrew Scriptures. I came to the conclusion that *ahavah* and *agape* are synonymous.

Subsequent to this study, I was reminded that before Jesus was born the Hebrew Scriptures were translated into Greek. This translation is known as the "Septuagint." It is a fact that the Greek language, along with Latin, was the common tongue of the Roman Empire, which included Israel. During Jesus' time many Jewish people were scattered throughout the Roman Empire, where Greek was used in business and government. Just as English speaking people today use English translations of the Bible, the Greek speaking Jewish people of the Roman Empire used the Septuagint. The Septuagint was so widely accepted and utilized that in practically every instance where the writers of the New Testament quoted the Old Testament they used the Septuagint. Since this is true, we know that the inspired authors were familiar with this Greek translation of the Hebrew Scriptures.

Prior to this, I had never researched how the translators of the Septuagint treated the Hebrew term for "love" (*ahavah*). Imagine my surprise when I found out that my conclusions were correct. Within the Greek translation of the Hebrew Scriptures, *ahavah* is consistently translated into Greek as *agape*; this occurs more than 200 times. Since we know that *agape* was widely utilized in the Septuagint, which was widely read by the Jewish community, we also know that the commonly held view of *agape's* history – that *agape* was a little known term being given a totally new meaning – is mistaken.

Marcionism and Gnosticism were two ancient heresies that greatly differed on many crucial things, but their arrogance found common ground in this: these systems taught that the God of the New Testament is superior to the God described in the Old Testament. In fact, it is absolutely true that the God of the Old Testament is the same God as the Father of our Lord Jesus the Messiah. This God *is agape* and has always acted consistently with His nature. There is no discontinuity between the love of the Old Testament and the love of the New Testament.

Whether through ignorance, or bias, the common understanding of *agape* ignores how it is used throughout the Septuagint.

Therefore, these popular definitions ignore the way the word was understood by the Jewish people who were living in the time of Jesus and the Apostles. This means the common understanding unintentionally ignores the way the authors of the New Testament viewed *agape* and intended *agape* to be understood when they wrote it!

## How *Agape* is Used in Scripture

Now that we have introduced the common understanding of *agape*, we will begin to look at how the word *agape* is used in the Scriptures. Determining how *agape* is used in Scripture will enable us to form a "Biblical definition." To do this we will look in both the New Testament and the Greek translation of the Old Testament, the Septuagint. Our utilizing the Septuagint will reveal a continuity of usage and will help us to more fully appreciate the intention of the New Testament writers as they employed the word *agape* in various contexts.

Let's rehearse a simple explanation of the common understanding, which is actually a misunderstanding, of *agape*. The common consensus is that *agape* is the highest form of love. It is completely different from human love. This love is not based upon the worth or value of the one being loved. Nor is it based on a desire or appreciation in the lover. *Agape* is based upon a choice to act lovingly, or the nature of the lover, and it happens regardless of the degree of merit or lack thereof in the one being loved.

Is this the kind of love we see in Scripture? As we go through these verses, compare this definition with what you see in the Bible. Determine if this definition is adequate – does it hold up? Or is *agape* in Scripture something else altogether? If you hold to the common understanding of *agape*, prepare for a paradigm shift.

As you read the following information, I implore you to carefully consider, meditate, and pray. Make room for the Holy Spirit to interact with your heart through the Scriptures. As you read through these verses in the New and Old Testaments, remember this: each time you read a word translated "love" you are reading a translation of the word *agape* (unless otherwise noted).

## *Agape* as an Emotion

The first thing we shall establish is that love is a feeling. Love is felt. In the following verses we see that *agape* is an emotion which is associated with other emotions, in particular the emotion of joy.

> You heard that I said to you, "I go away, and I will come to you." If you loved Me, you would have rejoiced because I go to the Father, for the Father is greater than I (John 14:28).

> But the fruit of the Spirit is love, joy, peace, patience, kindness, goodness, faithfulness (Galatians 5:22).

In the next verses, *agape* is contrasted with another, opposing emotion.

> Just as it is written, "Jacob I loved, but Esau I hated" (Romans 9:13).

> You have loved righteousness and hated lawlessness; therefore God, your God, has anointed you with the oil of gladness above your companions (Hebrews 1:9).

In the same way that hatred is a strong emotion, so is *agape*. It is written that God hates lawlessness. Does God have no visceral hatred of lawlessness? Is God's love without "feeling"? The following verses further illustrate that *agape* is an emotion which can be contrasted with other emotions.

## *Septuagint*

> If a man has two wives, the one loved and the other unloved, and both the loved and the unloved have borne him sons, if the first-born son belongs to the unloved, then it shall be in the day he wills

what he has to his sons, he cannot make the son of the loved the firstborn before the son of the unloved, who is the firstborn (Deuteronomy 21:15,16).

Hate evil, love good, and establish justice in the gate! Perhaps the LORD God of hosts may be gracious to the remnant of Joseph (Amos 5:15).

The word *agape* is used to convey the emotion of love, together with other emotions, and contrasted with other emotions.

## *Agape* as Wholehearted Devotional Emotional Love for God

And you shall love the Lord your God with all your heart, and with all your soul, and with all your mind, and with all your strength (Mark 12:30).

What is heart-worship like? "All your **heart**..." Does that sound devoid of emotion? *Agape* in this context means the release of devotion, affection, appreciation, desire, delight...in short, it means "love."

We can clearly see that God calls for more than the exercise of volition. He is calling us to love Him, not merely act, or determine to act, like we love Him. We are concentrating on a commandment, but love is not a cold decision. Love decides, love uses volition to pursue love's objectives, but *agape* is not merely an act of your will. Love is a feeling.

## *Septuagint*

Now, Israel, what does the LORD your God require from you, but to fear the LORD your God, to walk in all His ways and love Him, and to serve the LORD your God with all your heart and with all your soul (Deuteronomy 10:12).

O love the LORD, all you His godly ones! The LORD preserves the faithful and fully recompenses the proud doer (Psalm 31:23).

In this verse in Isaiah, the prophet is "singing" for his Beloved, the one he *agapes*. He's singing a poignant love song for God:

> Let me sing now for my well-beloved a song of my beloved concerning His vineyard. My well-beloved had a vineyard on a fertile hill (Isaiah 5:1).

*Agape* can describe wholehearted devotional love for God.

## *Agape* as Paternal Love

> [Abraham and Isaac] He said, "Take now your son, your only son, whom you love, Isaac, and go to the land of Moriah, and offer him there as a burnt offering on one of the mountains of which I will tell you" (Genesis 22:2).

Here we find the first mention of the word "love" *(ahavah/agape)* in the Bible. This story describes the deeply emotional, heartfelt love Abraham had for Isaac. It is in the light of this awesome attachment that the challenge is so clearly seen. This sacred story became the backdrop to the Father offering up His Son for the sins of the world.

> And a voice came out of the heavens: "You are My beloved Son, in You I am well-pleased" (Mark 1:11).

This is not describing a cold rational choice to act lovingly. No! This is a Father beaming with love, pride, and affirmation for His Son. Certainly there was something about Jesus that the Father really loved…really *agaped*, wasn't there? Jesus was phenomenally precious to Abba.

Jesus knew this and spoke of His Father's love for Him. Let's look at paternal love through the eyes of the Son.

> Father, I desire that they also, whom You have given Me, be with Me where I am, so that they may see My glory which You have given Me, for You loved Me before the foundation of the world (John 17:24).

> Just as the Father has loved Me, I have also loved you; abide in My love (John 15:9).

There is also paternal love in the Church.

> I do not write these things to shame you, but to admonish you as my beloved children (1 Corinthians 4:14).

> For this reason I have sent to you Timothy, who is my beloved and faithful child in the Lord (1 Corinthians 4:17).

## *Septuagint*

> Now Isaac loved Esau, because he had a taste for game, but Rebekah loved Jacob (Genesis 25:28).

> For whom the LORD loves He reproves, even as a father corrects the son in whom he delights (Proverbs 3:12).

*Agape* often denotes paternal love.

## *Agape* as Devoted Affection

> Now Jesus loved Martha and her sister and Lazarus (John 11:5).

This verse describes a deep, loving, devoted, affectionate friendship – Jesus enjoyed this family. He *agaped* them. In the midst of the family's heartbreak and the community's grief, observers looked at Jesus and commented:

> See how He loved him! (John 11:36b).

In this verse, *phileo* – synonymous with *agape* in John's Gospel – is used. How did Jesus *agape* Lazarus? *With affectionate devotion.* God displays the same loving friendship throughout the Scriptures. Look at this:

> From the standpoint of the gospel they are enemies for your sake, but from the standpoint of God's choice they are beloved for the sake of the fathers (Romans 11:28).

God has such affection for and devotion to the Patriarchs that He is affectionately devoted to their offspring, Israel.

Here's another verse which uses *agape* to convey the meaning of devoted affection:

> Having so fond an affection for you, we were well-pleased to impart to you not only the gospel of God but also our own lives, because you had become very dear (*agapetoi*) to us (1 Thessalonians 2:8).

## *Septuagint*

> Jonathan made David vow again because of his love for him, because he loved him as he loved his own life (1 Samuel 20:17).

We choose our friends. We pick them because of mutual regard, common interests and loyalty. We trust our friends; they always care about our wellbeing. A good friend can be more devoted than a brother. *Agape* can be employed to depict the devoted affection of friends.

## Consider

The weakness of the common understanding of *agape* can be illustrated by the following: Suppose you're in a room and the most wonderful person is singing in a perfect voice the most beautiful love song ever written. You listen to the wonderful person's voice, you are inspired by the lyrics, the melody is powerful, the rhythm is moving you…

Only one thing stands in the way of your complete enjoyment of this song. It's not being sung specifically to you. You're getting the benefit of the song, but the beauty is in the words, the melody, the voice. The singer would be singing whether you were in the room or not.

Biblical *agape*'s song is different. God is singing a very personal song directly to you. You're hearing a song with your name in it. The singer is drawing near to you, leaning towards you, gazing into your eyes and singing to you. It's not just a wonderful singer singing a wonderful song. In Biblical *agape*'s song, the Lover is singing for a reason and He's singing to someone. He's singing because He's in love. He's singing to you, His true love. Can you hear His song? It's for you!

1.  What is the most important truth you learned in this chapter?

2.  Based on the categories of *agape* we have covered in this chapter, write a short definition of what Biblical *agape* looks like. Is this different from the view of *agape* you held before starting this book? If so describe the difference between your view and the Scripture's use of the word.

3.  Please read Zephaniah 3:17:

    > The LORD your God is in your midst, a victorious warrior. He will exult over you with joy, He will be quiet in His love, He will rejoice over you with shouts of joy.

    Paraphrase this verse and then describe in your own words what God's love looks like here.

4.  Choose one verse from the chapter which really spoke to your view of *agape*. Write some of your thoughts about the way *agape* is used in that verse.

5.  What did you struggle with the most in this chapter? Consider taking further time to study the Scriptures about this topic, and commit it to prayer.

6.  Please paraphrase, personalize and pray through 1 John 4:16:

    > We have come to know and have believed the love which God has for us. God is love, and the one who abides in love abides in God, and God abides in him.

*To love is to be emotionally invested in something; in Scripture this invest-ment includes caring for or serving the object of love.*

WALTER C. KAISER, ET. AL., *The Hard Sayings of the Bible*

*To love at all is to be vulnerable. Love anything and your heart will certainly be wrung and possibly broken…The alternative to tragedy, or at least to the risk of tragedy, is damnation. The only place outside of heaven where you can be perfectly safe from all dangers and perturbations of love is hell.*

C. S. LEWIS, *The Four Loves*

*What I believe is so magnificent, so glorious, that it is beyond finite compre-hension. To believe that the universe was created by a purposeful, benign Creator is one thing. To believe that this Creator took on human vesture, accepted death and mortality, was tempted, betrayed, broken, and all for love of us, defies reason. It is so wild that it terrifies some Christians who try to dogmatize their fear by lashing out at other Christians, because tidy Chris-tianity with all answers given is easier than one which reaches out to the wild wonder of God's love, a love we don't even have to earn.*

MADELEINE L'ENGLE

*Love is the irresistible desire to be irresistibly desired.*

MARK TWAIN

## Chapter 7

# The Array of *Agape*

*Yet the LORD longs to be gracious to you; He rises to show you compassion. For the LORD is a God of justice. Blessed are all who wait for Him! (Isaiah 30:18).*

IN THE LAST CHAPTER we began examining Scripture with the goal of developing a "Biblical definition" of the word *agape* (love). We defined the common understanding of *agape* as: "the highest form of love which is completely different from what human love is like. This love is not based upon the worth, or value of the one being loved. Nor is it based on a desire or appreciation in the person who is actively loving. Instead, *agape* is based upon a choice to act lovingly, and it happens regardless of the merit or lack of merit in the one being loved." Our goal is to see if this definition holds up when we really examine *agape* in the Scriptures.

So what have we seen in Scripture so far? We've seen that *agape* means the emotion of love. It is sometimes combined with other emotions, like joy. At other times it is contrasted with emotions like hatred or bitterness.

*Agape* can also describe wholehearted loving devotion towards God. Loving devotion involves all the faculties of our hearts, all that we are. This is more than just choosing to act lovingly towards God.

*Agape* can denote deep devoted affection between friends. Examples of this include David and Jonathan, and Jesus and Lazarus. Jonathan gave up his own chance at the throne because of his devotion to David. Jesus' devoted *agape* for Lazarus was apparent to all as He wept at His friend Lazarus' grave (John 11:5,11,35). Let's recall that John was called the "disciple whom Jesus loved." There was obviously a devoted affection between that disciple and the Messiah.

*Agape* can describe the deep love of a father for his son. We can have no doubt that Abraham's love for his long awaited son Isaac was deep, tender, and strong, as is the Father's love for Jesus.

How does this all compare to the common understanding of *agape*? So far we see that the common understanding and the way *agape* is used in Scripture are two completely different things. Let's continue looking at *agape* in the Bible. We have a lot more ground to cover, so let's go on with our study.

### *Agape* as Love Which is Common to Humanity

Rather than being something alien to humanity, Scriptural *agape* can describe love which is common to all mankind. In what circumstances can a normal human being show *agape*? Here's an example: there was a centurion who *agaped* Israel.

> For he loves our nation and it was he who built us our synagogue (Luke 7:5).

The truth is that humanity can, and does, love with a love described as *agape*. In fact, Jesus disclosed that tax collectors – traitors – can *agape*.

> For if you love those who love you, what reward do you have? Do not even the tax collectors do the same? (Matthew 5:46)

Surprisingly, even sinners *agape*! There is a natural affection in mankind. *Agape* can mean natural affection.

> If you love those who love you, what credit is that to you? For even sinners love those who love them (Luke 6:32).

This natural affection can exist even in hell. Though *agape* is not used in these verses, note the natural affection that exists in this story. This is an example of "loving those who love you."

> And he said, "Then I beg you, father, that you send him to my father's house – for I have five brothers – in order that he may warn them, so that they will not also come to this place of torment" (Luke 16:27–28).

*Agape* is common to all men.

## *Agape* for a Reason

The common understanding of *agape* is that it is either a totally free act of one's volition or is the overflow of a loving nature. Thus, *agape* is not caused or bestowed for a reason. Yet, these verses describe *agape* being given for a reason.

> For this reason the Father loves Me, because I lay down My life so that I may take it again (John 10:17).

Jesus saw Himself as *agaped* because of His actions and attitude. Don't you think He was correct? Didn't Father see someone worth loving when He considered His Son's character, personality and way of life?

> Each one must do just as he has purposed in his heart, not grudgingly or under compulsion, for God loves a cheerful giver (2 Corinthians 9:7).

Here, Paul exhorts believers to contribute to the needs of others because it will please God. The action and attitude of "cheerful giving" gives God joy and inspires Him to *agape* the giver.

## *Agape* Because of Gratitude

One reason for *agape* is gratitude. Again, *agape* can be a response to another's actions. This is a love which can be provoked. In the following verse *agape* is used to describe a spontaneous expression of gratitude.

> A moneylender had two debtors: one owed five hundred denarii, and the other fifty. When they were unable to repay, he graciously forgave them both. ***So which of them will love him more?*** (Luke 7:41–42).

Another reason for *agape* is – *agape*! Amazingly, in this verse, *agape* is seen as being something that can be provoked by *agape* – almost a reciprocal *agape*.

> I will most gladly spend and be expended for your souls. If I love you more, am I to be loved less? (2 Corinthians 12:15).

*Agape* can be for various reasons.

## *Agape* of Differing Strengths

This should not surprise us, but since *agape* has been idealized and absolutized it may come as a shock to some to realize that not all *agape* is "equal." *Agape* can occur in varying degrees of intensity. Returning to 2 Corinthians 12:15, we see that it also talks about love of differing intensities. Let's read it again:

> I will most gladly spend and be expended for your souls. If I love you more, am I to be loved less? (2 Corinthians 12:15)

Here is another verse which speaks of a specific magnitude of *agape*.

> But God, being rich in mercy, because of His great love with which He loved us" (Ephesians 2:4).

The presence of the term "great" indicates that this love can occur in various strengths. No doubt, God is merciful and loving to all of Creation. However, He has great *agape* with which He has *agaped* us!

> For out of much affliction and anguish of heart I wrote to you with many tears; not so that you would be made sorrowful, but that you might know the love which I have especially for you (2 Corinthians 2:4).

*Thayer's Lexicon* defines this word *perissos* as "in a greater degree; more earnestly, more exceedingly" and in this verse used as "especially, above others." *Agape* can be especially for someone in contrast to someone else who is *agaped* less.

## Septuagint

> Now Israel loved Joseph more than all his sons, because he was the son of his old age; and he made him a varicolored tunic (Genesis 37:3).

> I love *(agape)* those who love *(phileo)* me; and those who diligently seek me will find me (Proverbs 8:17).

*Agape* can be in varying degrees: more or less, great love, love especially for someone.

## *Agape* as Marital Love

> As He says also in Hosea, "I will call those who were not My people, 'My people,' and her who was not beloved, 'Beloved' " (Romans 9:25).

> Husbands, love your wives, just as Christ also loved the church and gave Himself up for her (Ephesians 5:25).

> Husbands, love your wives and do not be embittered against them (Colossians 3:19).

I have often heard that in Ephesians 5:25 Paul was exhorting husbands to make a decision to act lovingly. It is a common catchphrase that within marriage *agape* is not a feeling but an act of will. Yet, in Colossians 3 *agape* is contrasted with another word, "embittered." To this day I've never heard anyone say that bitterness was not a "feeling." *Agape* in marriage is an emotion.

My wife doesn't want me to act as if I care about her because I have great control over my volition and want to do the right thing. Neither would she be content if she experienced love simply because I am a loving person. My wife actually wants me to love her.

## *Septuagint*

> (first time for marital love in Scriptures) Then Isaac brought her into his mother Sarah's tent, and he took Rebekah, and she became his wife, and he loved her; thus Isaac was comforted after his mother's death (Genesis 24:67).

> So Jacob served seven years for Rachel and they seemed to him but a few days because of his love for her (Genesis 29:20).

> (Longing for *agape*) Leah conceived and bore a son and named him Reuben, for she said, "Because the LORD has seen my affliction; surely now my husband will love me" (Genesis 29:32).

*Agape* can portray marital love.

## *Agape* **for the Wrong Things**

It may be hard to believe, but it is possible for us to *agape* a lot of bad things.

> No one can serve two masters; for either he will hate the one and love the other, or he will be devoted to one and despise the other. You cannot serve God and wealth (Matthew 6:24).

> For they loved the approval of men rather than the approval of God (John 12:43).

> This is the judgment, that the Light has come into the world, and men loved the darkness rather than the Light, for their deeds were evil (John 3:19).

> For Demas, having loved this present world, has deserted me and gone to Thessalonica; Crescens has gone to Galatia, Titus to Dalmatia (2 Timothy 4:10).

> Do not love the world nor the things in the world. If anyone loves the world, the love of the Father is not in him (1 John 2:15).

Forsaking the right way, they have gone astray, having followed the way of Balaam, the son of Beor, who loved the wages of unrighteousness (2 Peter 2:15).

## *Septuagint*

The LORD tests the righteous and the wicked, and the one who loves violence His soul hates (Psalm 11:5).

Your rulers are rebels and companions of thieves; everyone loves a bribe and chases after rewards. They do not defend the orphan, nor does the widow's plea come before them (Isaiah 1:23).

The prophets prophesy falsely, and the priests rule on their own authority; and My people love it so! But what will you do at the end of it? (Jeremiah 5:31).

A merchant, in whose hands are false balances, he loves to oppress (Hosea 12:7).

What are these things some men *agape*?

They *agape* the approval of men

They *agape* mammon

They *agape* darkness

They *agape* this present cosmos

They *agape* the wages of unrighteousness

They *agape* violence, bribery, an apostate status quo, oppression

Let's ask a further question here…Why do they *agape* these things?

They *agape* them because they see them as deserving of their love – these things are lovely to them. They perceive them as worthy objects of their affection. They are attracted to them.

## Chapter Summary

*Agape* in the Bible is used to describe a lot of different aspects of love.

Paternal love

Devotion to God

Devoted affection between friends

Natural love

Emotional love

Marital love

Love in varying degrees

Love for the wrong things

In addition, we see that the Bible uses *agape* to speak of love:

From God to Jesus

From God to man

From man to God

From man to man (even fallen man!)

From man to things

Remember, the common concept of *agape* is divine, volitional, unconditional, disinterested, unattached, unmotived "love." Do we find this borne out in Scripture? Quite the opposite. The *agape* of the Bible is: vibrant, intense, attached, affectionate, emotional, and very earthy. It is what we normally think of when we think of love. Rather than some hyper-spiritual, remote and unattainable attribute, the love of the Bible, *agape*, is true love.

## Consider

One of the most intense illustrations of love and commitment upon which one can meditate is the "Binding of Isaac." God called Abraham to sacrifice Isaac as a burnt offering. We find in the Torah that a burnt offering was not merely killed and burnt; it was killed, gutted, had its limbs cut off, and was then burned to ashes. "Offer your beloved son up as a burnt offering. Butcher your child."

The familiarity of this story immunizes us to the initial horror Abraham must have felt. When we take this call seriously we gasp at the demand, "What father could do that to the only son he loved?"

When we consider that God actually did that for us at Golgotha, it's awe-provoking. God gave His only begotten Son Whom He loved – on our behalf.

See how great a love the Father has bestowed on us (1 John 3:1a).

This is intense, astonishing, unfathomable love. Have you seen the love of God for you at Calvary?

1. What is the most important truth you learned in this chapter?

2. Read the following verse about *agape* for the wrong things:

   Woe to you Pharisees! For you love the chief seats in the synagogues and the respectful greetings in the market places (Luke 11:43).

   What does the ability to *agape* the wrong things tell you about the nature of *agape*?

3. Do you find *agape* for the wrong things in your own heart?

4. *Agape* in Scripture describes various aspects of human love. Consider your feelings for someone you really love. What aspects of love do you find within your own heart?

   This exercise can give you an indication of the way God feels towards you. Take what you've written about your love for others and deliberately apply it to God's heart towards you. Write down one aspect of your love for others which stretches your faith about God's love for you. Why is it a struggle to believe?

5.  What did you struggle with the most in this chapter? Consider taking further time to study the Scriptures about this topic, and commit it to prayer.

6.  Please paraphrase, personalize and pray through Isaiah 30:18:

    Yet the LORD longs to be gracious to you; He rises to show you compassion. For the LORD is a God of justice. Blessed are all who wait for Him!

*Would God command us to love in a way that He does not?*
*Would God demand that our love be more far reaching than His own?*

JOHN MACARTHUR, JR.

*He has paid us the intolerable compliment of loving us, in the deepest, most tragic, most inexorable sense.*

C. S. LEWIS

*[Christ] is the breathing forth of the heart, life and spirit of God into all the dead race of Adam. He is the seeker, the finder, the restorer of all that, from Cain to the end of time, was lost and dead to the life of God. He is the love that prays for all its murderers; the love that willingly suffers and dies among thieves, that thieves may have a life with him in Paradise; the love that visits publicans, harlots and sinners, and wants and seeks to forgive where most is to be forgiven.*

WILLIAM LAW

*The love of God…is unlimited and constant, but we know it in increasing measure when we accept it for what it is and grow into a deeper understanding and experience of it.*

CARL KINBAR

# Chapter 8

# What is God's Love Like?

*When He approached Jerusalem, He saw the city and wept over it (Luke 19:41).*

IN CHAPTERS SIX AND SEVEN WE ASKED: "How does the Bible use the word *agape* (love)?" This began to provide a Biblical understanding of "love." Through exploring Scripture, we found that the love of the Bible is vibrant, intense, attached, affectionate, emotional, and very earthy; it is true love.

Now, let's ask a further question: What is God's *agape* like? Let's start where we left off with the examination of *agape*. Our overall contention is that the *agape* of the Bible is true love. What is true love? True love is real, honest, pure, enduring, faithful, and sincere love. When we contend that God's love is true love, we are ascribing all of these qualities to it. We are saying that God's love is not a pretense. It is not false, hypocritical, artificial or illusory. It is genuine, and precisely what the word "love" implies: God's love is truly love.

Now, so far you might be thinking, "Well of course God's love is true love. Of course it is real love." Yet, as with the Greek word *agape*, many believers have a concept of God's love that is very unlike what we find in the Scriptures. As with *agape* in general, many see God's love as a high, holy, ethical, and detached love, something devoid of emotion and not very love-like.

## Common Misconceptions

Here are some common misconceptions about the love of God.

Many mistakenly believe that although God wouldn't love *you*, per se, He would *treat* you like He loves you because of what Jesus has done for you, but not because He means it. In this view He doesn't really love *you*, but you can experience what being loved by God feels like for Jesus' sake.

Others misplace *agape* completely within the province of the will. Since He is altogether good, wonderful, and perfect, He makes a moral decision to do what is right: to "love" us. In this view, His love is an ethical choice and bears little resemblance to what we know as love.

Still others maintain that God's *agape* is "unconditional love." According to this view, you didn't earn His love and you can never lose it; there's nothing you are and nothing you can do to make God love you, either more or less. It's just a fixed state or a steady flow. In this view, once again, the "love" is not really about you at all. You're not experiencing love because you are beloved or lovely, but because it is God's nature to love.

The problem with these concepts is this: they have nothing to do with the objects of God's love. In each instance, God's love is not based on appreciation, attraction, emotion, delight, and desire, but on something else. These concepts just don't measure up to the love of the Bible – vibrant, intense, attached, affectionate, emotional, and very earthy! The love of the Bible is what we would think of as love, what we experience as love; this is also the reality with God's love. It is true love.

Before we begin looking at specific aspects of the love God has for you, let's look at some evidence of a vibrant, intense, attached, affectionate, emotional (true!) love in God's heart for *you*.

# How We Know His Love is True

## The Call to Wholehearted Devotion

One way we know God's love is true love is that He calls us to wholehearted love and devotion. For a moment, suppose our *agape* towards God could be assayed and measured like gold. Gold's purity is often measured by "karats." Pure gold is described as "twenty-four karat gold." If a person purchases a ring that is eighteen karat gold, the percentage of gold in the ring is seventy-five percent. It also means that there are six karats of other base metals (twenty-five percent) in the ring. Twenty-four karat gold is called "fine gold." It is unalloyed. The nature of our hearts' *agape* towards God is to be pure and unalloyed, whole and not adulterated. Answer this, is it conceivable that we are called to love God with a higher quality of love than the love with which He loves us?

> And you shall love the Lord your God with all your heart, and with all your soul, and with all your mind, and with all your strength (Mark 12:30).

He commands, "Love Me with all of your heart, with all of your soul, with all of your mind, with all of your strength." We're being called to get really involved. Not just, love Him with your heart, and mind, etc., but *"with all of your..."* This is an intense verse. Yet some would have us believe His love is disinterested, unattached, and essentially indifferent to those called to experience His love. How can this be?

Those who think God is not emotionally involved with His people are wrong. The testimony of the prophets is that God's love is utterly wholehearted. Jeremiah prophesied that His restorative activity is carried out with all of the zealous love of which He is capable.

> I will rejoice over them to do them good and will faithfully plant them in this land with all My heart and with all My soul (Jeremiah 32:41).

He loves us in the same way that we are called to love Him. The Lord is saying, "I love you with all of My heart, with all of My soul, all of My mind, all of My strength. Return this same love to Me. It is my desire that we would be equally yoked. Love Me in this way."

God is after a reciprocal relationship. That's what the passion of Jesus is about. God Incarnate demonstrates a love so great that it is willing to sweat, suffer, and be agonizingly sacrificed on behalf of the beloved. The beloved is prized so much that the Lover is willing to do absolutely anything for the object of His love.

## The Royal Law

Another indicator that His love is authentic can be found in the "Royal Law." What is this law and what does it tell us about the King? The Royal Law is found in James 2:8:

> If you really keep the Royal Law found in Scripture, "Love your neighbor as yourself," you are doing right.

Our King has given us a law. This law is a picture of the King's heart. This Royal Law is a revelation of God's love. God wants us to actually love the people around us. Why? Because *He* loves them and wants them to be loved. This law is not just a means to regulate our lives. It is the cry of God's heart.

Let's look further: with what type of love are we called to love one another?

> Since you have in obedience to the truth purified your souls for a *sincere* love of the brethren, *fervently* love one another from the heart (1 Peter 1:22).

> Above all, keep *fervent* in your love for one another, because love covers a multitude of sins (1 Peter 4:8).

This call to earnest unfeigned love of the brethren conveys God's heart of true love. We're commanded to fervently and sincerely love one another. He's not calling us to love in a way which is completely different than His own love. These verses reveal something to us about the love of God: His love for us is sincere. His love is fervent. His love is sincerely fervent.

## God's Hatred of Insincerity

One thing in Scripture, perhaps more than any other, speaks to us about the genuine quality of God's love: God abhors insincere love. The following is God's response to insincerity:

> You hypocrites, rightly did Isaiah prophesy of you: "This people honors me with their lips, but their heart is far away from Me. But in vain do they worship Me, teaching as doctrine the precepts of men" (Matthew 15:7–9).

Your King is not satisfied with acts of worship that mimic true devotion. (Why should anyone be satisfied with that type of love?) How can anyone imagine our Creator would be content to love us in the way He despises being "loved"?! God is not a hypocrite. His love is intense. His love is more than an act of His will. His love is more than a benevolent unconditional manifestation of a loving heart. God's love is true love.

## The Reality Demonstrated: the Son

The greatest revelation of God's love was given when Father exposed His very heart: His Son. Please read John 1:18:

> No one has seen God at any time; the only begotten God who is in the bosom of the Father, He has explained Him.

This Son, "who was in the bosom of the Father," exposed God's heart. God's heart vulnerably drew near to us. We responded. This heart was brutalized, rejected and crucified. Yet God used this rejection as the means to forgive our sins. Why? He "covers the multitude of (our) sins" (1 Peter 4:8) to deal with the alienation between us. He wants a relationship with us. At the cost of His blood He covers our sins which separate us from Him because He values us more than He hates our offenses against Him. The crucifixion of Jesus is an incredible indicator of a deep and genuine love.

## Anthropomorphic Language

When we read a portion of Scripture which describes God as if He were human, or doing something human, we are reading anthropomorphic language. For instance, when one reads about God having "eyes," this is an anthropomorphism. When we read about God having a human role in Psalm 23, "The LORD is my shepherd," we are reading an anthropomorphism. Yet, many people speak of anthropomorphisms as if they are conveying something which is untrue. Let's test this against 2 Timothy 3:16–17:

> All Scripture is inspired by God and profitable for teaching, for reproof, for correction, for training in righteousness; so that the man of God may be adequate, equipped for every good work.

"*All* Scripture is inspired by God and profitable." God didn't make a mistake by including anthropomorphic language in the Bible. Anthropomorphisms are the Spirit's attempt to help us understand something about God. For instance, in the same way we hear, God hears, only more. More. He hears *more*! Here is an example from Scripture:

> Just as a father has compassion on his children, so the LORD has compassion on those who fear Him (Psalm 103:13).

He will have *more* compassion. His heart will respond like a loving Father – *more!*

Anthropomorphic language in the Scriptures is highly revelatory. In it we receive an understanding of God to which we can relate, and yet it conveys something beyond us: a father's compassion – *more*! This is the God we serve.

Let's look at Psalm 94:8–10:

> Pay heed, you senseless among the people; and when will you understand, stupid ones? He who planted the ear, does He not hear? He who formed the eye, does He not see? He who chastens the nations, will He not rebuke, even He who teaches man knowledge?

This verse delivers a strong reproof for those who choose to refuse God's communication through anthropomorphic language: "when will you understand, stupid ones?" God is saying, "These things speak of Me! The ear speaks of My hearing. The eye speaks of My seeing."

Now, permit me to add my own "does He not" question to this list:

### *He who created the heart, does He not love?*

Certainly, the God Who created the heart of man feels, surely He loves. He gave us the capacity to feel and to love, and this speaks of His own capacity. Just as He sees more, just as He hears more, He also feels more, He also loves more! Anthropomorphic language can serve as a powerful testimony of the love of God for us.

## Review

Let's briefly review how far we've come. We are seeking to establish that God's love is a true love. It is not an imitation love. It is not the semblance of love without the reality of the heart of love. It is not a fake or a look-alike. It is real love. This is clearly attested to in

Scripture. It is seen in His commands to us. It is seen in His hatred of insincerity. It is seen in the way He created us to love. It is seen in the extraordinary gift of His Son. It is seen in anthropomorphic language. He loves us with an authentic love.

## Aspects of this True Love

Now that we've established that God's love for us is true, let's look at some specific aspects of what this love is like.

### Attraction

Just as we discovered when defining *agape*, attraction is a root motivation of love. We love what we find lovely. Amazingly, God loves what He finds lovely, too.

When we look at the Scriptures we find that *agape* can easily be defined as "love because of the perceived worth of the object loved." At the risk of being facetious, you experience *agape* when you "love" something. You love something when you perceive the "thing" loved as "lovely," or "lovable" – worth loving.

We are lovely to God; to God we are worth loving. Let's look at some verses:

> Jesus looked at him and loved him (Mark 10:21a).

> God saw all that He had made, and behold, it was very good. And there was evening and there was morning, the sixth day (Genesis 1:31).

When Jesus looked at the rich young ruler, He was not repulsed by what He saw. He loved this man, misguided and entangled as he was. When God looked at Creation (including humanity), He didn't turn away in frustration or disappointment. He looked, He evaluated, He found it to be good. Our Creator is holy, majestic, omniscient and all-wise. God has more than enough skill and power to create anything He wants. He is no fool. And He loves us; He finds us lovely! Attraction to (and appreciation for) humanity is one aspect of God's love.

## God's Love is Emotional

Another aspect of God's love is that it is emotional. God's love is not just a product of His willpower or the expression of a wonderful nature, it is a feeling. Some in their interest to maintain the concept of God as perfect (needing nothing) distance His emotions from His creation. To them, God remains unattached and disinterested. To them, He is "God the Great Stoic."

Does Scripture speak to this mentality? Let's look at a passage:

> When He approached Jerusalem, He saw the city and wept over it, saying, "If you had known in this day, even you, the things which make for peace! But now they have been hidden from your eyes. For the days will come upon you when your enemies will throw up a barricade against you, and surround you and hem you in on every side, and they will level you to the ground and your children within you, and they will not leave in you one stone upon another, because you did not recognize the time of your visitation" (Luke 19:41–44).

Look, there's Jesus convulsively weeping, gasping for breath, snot running down His beard, over the coming judgment of Jerusalem. Is Jesus demonstrating His emotional distance from His creation? Is this the reserved and unaffected One? One of the Divine Names is not "Jehovah Stoic."

The Greek word used for "weeping" in this verse is *klaio*. Have you ever seen a broken hearted child? Have you ever mourned to the extent you could not help wailing and sobbing aloud? *Klaio* conveys these thoughts. Jesus was moved; He felt real grief over Jerusalem. He actually emotionally loved Israel!

This is not just manifest in the Incarnation. It is the testimony of the prophets.

> How can I give you up, O Ephraim? How can I surrender you, O Israel? How can I make you like Admah? How can I treat you like Zeboiim? My heart is turned over within Me, all My compassions are kindled (Hosea 11:8).

Is God stoic? Impossible. The testimony of Scripture is that God is an emotional God. He deeply feels: love, joy, passion, grief, even anger. And if you're tempted to say, "Oh, that's just anthropomorphic language," remember, when it comes to talking about God, anthropomorphic language conveys something true, only *more*. If it's "only" anthropomorphic language, then we are to see that God loves *more*, God grieves *more*, God cares *more*. God's love for you is a deeply emotional love.

## God's Love is Ardent

Taking this concept of emotional love a step further, we can say that God's love is ardent love. It's a fiery love, a passionate love. The image of God as the passionate lover or husband is present throughout the Scriptures. It was sanctified graphically in the Song of Songs, which uses *agape* nineteen times in the Septuagint. This aspect of love is continued as a theme in the prophets, detailed in Ephesians 5, and celebrated in Revelation. It's a picture of the culmination of history. It represents the reason God created humanity in the first place. He always had a plan, and marriage portrays this plan.

God has revealed that there is an aspect of His *agape* which can only be glimpsed through romantic love. He desires humanity spiritually (not physically) in a way that corresponds to a young man in the prime of his life ardently desiring the bride of his dreams.

With an emotionally mature young man this includes the pleasure of her company. With a physically healthy young man it goes beyond friendship. Romantic love in its fullest human expression corresponds to God's spiritual desire in the same manner that human sight corresponds to a God Who sees.

Some assert this revelation is for sisters, but I think this revelation might be especially relevant for men as well. Brothers, perhaps the same type of ardent longing you've experienced is going on in God towards *you*. Men, have you ever seen God as someone who is ardently longing for you? Meditate upon that thought for a while.

> And as the bridegroom rejoices over the bride, so your God will rejoice over you (Isaiah 62:5b).

## God's Ardent Love Produces Jealousy

In addition, God is jealous over His people's love, attention, and devotion. This jealousy may provoke His wrath and ultimately makes His wrath a derivation of His love and intense desire. The Lord's jealousy is not just an Old Testament concept. Although this may make us uncomfortable, it is still true. Look at how James portrays this:

> Or do you think that the Scripture speaks to no purpose: "He jealously desires the spirit which He has made to dwell in us"? (James 4:5).

Here's a little story:

Imagine the return of a victorious warrior. The enemy had determined to undermine and destroy his family. The warrior defeated his enemy's army for the sake of his family at great expense and utterly exhausting effort. Look, there's the blood of his enemies mingled with his own, spattered over his clothing. He's returning, victorious, from the field of battle.

> Why is Your apparel red, and Your garments like the one who treads in the winepress? "I have trodden the wine trough alone, and from

> the peoples there was no man with Me. I also trod them in My anger and trampled them in My wrath; and their lifeblood is sprinkled on My garments, and I stained all My raiment. For the day of vengeance was in My heart, and My year of redemption has come" (Isaiah 63:2–4).

He opens the door to his home only to find his wife, the light of his eyes, in the lascivious mocking embrace of his enemy, giving herself unashamedly, ignoring the warrior at the door and asking him to shut it on his way out.

> You adulteresses, do you not know that friendship with the world is hostility toward God? Therefore whoever wishes to be a friend of the world makes himself an enemy of God. Or do you think that the Scripture speaks to no purpose: "He jealously desires the spirit which He has made to dwell in us"? (James 4:4–5).

If, after all He has done, she still refuses to return to Him, how do you think such a warrior would act? What would the response of that warrior be?

> Thus I will judge you like women who commit adultery or shed blood are judged; and I will bring on you the blood of wrath and jealousy (Ezekiel 16:38).

Humanity is ransomed through the blood of the victorious death and war of the Messiah. Jesus has ascended to heaven and yet He's standing at the door, knocking. Meanwhile the object of His devotion, humanity for which He died, makes love to His worst enemy. Jesus responds with wrath and jealousy. He is ardently longing for them, and therefore He will war against that which steals them away. The Lord will destroy the root and results of sin (spiritual adultery) which separate them from Him. This jealousy comes out of *agape*. It is not antithetical to love; it is a zealous derivative and demonstration of the *agape* that sent Him to the cross. Our God loves us with an ardent, jealous love.

Does this help you understand this aspect of the Biblical language of wrath? The power and depth of this jealousy makes the most intense desire and jealousy of which we are capable resemble a shadow's substance. We see this zeal in its awesome fury at the cross when Jesus took our place and bore the wrath of God. God could not stand to see us in the devil's embrace, so He expended all of His effort in one awesome sacrifice. He paid for our sins, broke our chains, and has received the restored love of His bride.

Ultimately this victorious outcome is reflected in the prophecy of Zephaniah 3:

> "Therefore wait for Me," declares the LORD, "for the day when I rise up as a witness. Indeed, My decision is to gather nations, to assemble kingdoms, to pour out on them My indignation, all My burning anger; for all the earth will be devoured by the fire of My zeal. For then I will give to the peoples purified lips, that all of them may call on the name of the LORD, to serve Him shoulder to shoulder."...Shout for joy, O daughter of Zion! Shout in triumph, O Israel! Rejoice and exult with all your heart, O daughter of Jerusalem! The LORD has taken away His judgments against you; He has cleared away your enemies. The King of Israel, the LORD, is in your midst; you will fear disaster no more. In that day it will be said to Jerusalem: "Do not be afraid, O Zion; do not let your hands fall limp. The LORD your God is in your midst, a victorious warrior. *He will exult over you with joy, He will be quiet in His love, He will rejoice over you with shouts of joy*" (Zephaniah 3:8,9,14–17).

This is the ardent love which moved the prophets to speak. This is the jealous love which sent His Son to die. This is the longing love which sends the Church into the world to demonstrate and proclaim the Gospel of the Kingdom. This love will ultimately be victorious at the return of the Lord Jesus.

## God's Love is Such that He Delights in Our Love

Let me ask you a few questions. How does God respond to those who love Him? What does that tell us about Him? What does that tell us about His love for us?

> Blessed is the man who perseveres under trial, because when he has stood the test, he will receive the crown of life that God has promised to those who love Him (James 1:12).

> Listen, my dear brothers: Has not God chosen those who are poor in the eyes of the world to be rich in faith and to inherit the kingdom He promised those who love Him? (James 2:5).

> But if anyone loves God, he is known by Him (1 Corinthians 8:3).

There is a reward for those who love God. He intends to give us the crown of life, to give us the kingdom as our inheritance. He takes special notice of those who love Him. This speaks of the delight God has in those who love Him. He not only loves us, He loves our love for Him! His delight in our love for Him produces a response from His heart. In fact, Jesus has gone to prepare a place for us:

> If I go and prepare a place for you, I will come again and receive you to Myself, that where I am, there you may be also (John 14:2b–3).

According to His rights as King, in harmony with His wisdom, for His pleasure – God has decided to bless those who love Him.

> But just as it is written, "things which eye has not seen and ear has not heard, and which have not entered the heart of man, all that God has prepared for those who love Him" (1 Corinthians 2:9).

Amazingly, God's love for us is such that He appreciates, enjoys, and actively reciprocates our love. For those who love Him, God stores up ways to demonstrate His love. He desires to communicate this love in ways we understand. Like everyone who loves, He wants His love to be known and appreciated by the beloved – the object of His love.

God's love is supposed to delight us like this verse:

> Let him kiss me with the kisses of his mouth – for your love is more delightful than wine (Song of Songs 1:2).

Our love delights God like this verse:

> You have made my heart beat faster, my sister, my bride; you have made my heart beat faster with a single glance of your eyes, with a single strand of your necklace (Song of Solomon 4:9).

In the same way He draws near to those who draw near to Him (James 4:8), so He responds to our love out of great joy and is storing up lavish expressions of appreciation. God's love is such that He delights in our love.

## Other Aspects of God's Love

The aspects of God's love which we have covered are in no way an exhaustive list. In fact, we could reexamine and expand many of the topics we covered in the prior chapters and find that these things are true of God's love. For instance, God's love is **paternal**.

> And a voice came out of the heavens: "You are My beloved Son, in You I am well-pleased" (Mark 1:11).

> If you then, being evil, know how to give good gifts to your children, how much more will your Father who is in heaven give what is good to those who ask Him! (Matthew 7:11).

God's love is **affectionately devoted**; He loves us as friends.

> Now Jesus loved (*agape*) Martha and her sister and Lazarus (John 11:5).

> And (Abraham) was called the friend (*philos*) of God (James 2:23b).

> Abraham My friend (*agape*) (Isaiah 41:8b).

We also find that God loves **for a reason**.

> For the Father Himself loves you, because you have loved Me and have believed that I came forth from the Father (John 16:27).

Basically, when we explore the Scriptures, we find out that God's love is wonderfully **true**. It is an intense, dynamic, deep, affectionate, and attached love which is for you!

## God's Love is Personal

Not only is God's love genuine, but it is **very** personal.

Paul often spoke of both a personal and corporate aspect of our relationship with God. For instance, Paul speaks of the temple in both corporate and individual terms.

> [Corporate] – Do you not know that you (plural) are a temple of God, and that the Spirit of God dwells in you (plural)? (1 Corinthians 3:16–17).

> [Individual] – Or do you not know that your body is a temple of the Holy Spirit who is in you, whom you have from God, and that you are not your own? (1 Corinthians 6:19).

He speaks of Jesus' sacrifice for us in much the same way, both corporately and individually. Messiah died for the world, He died for me.

> [Corporate] – namely, that God was in Christ reconciling the world to Himself, not counting their trespasses against them, and He has committed to us the word of reconciliation (2 Corinthians 5:19).

> [Individual] – Who loved me and gave Himself for me (Galatians 2:20b).

Paul saw himself as individually loved by Messiah. He knew that Jesus had premeditatedly, passionately sacrificed Himself for Paul. This is not a "corporate" understanding of God's love. It's individual, it's personal.

Other verses testify to this personalized love and care:

> But the very hairs of your head are all numbered (Matthew 10:30).

This verse is not referring to God's omniscience. It is an anthropomorphism. Imagine someone loving you enough to not only count but to itemize every hair on your head. The Lord not only knows the sum, but He has assigned each hair a number. That's a picture of God's love for you.

Speaking of things that can't be numbered, please read these verses:

> Many, O LORD my God, are the wonders which You have done, and Your thoughts toward us; there is none to compare with You. If I would declare and speak of them, they would be too numerous to count (Psalm 40:5).

> How precious also are Your thoughts to me, O God! How vast is the sum of them! If I should count them, they would outnumber the sand. When I awake, I am still with You (Psalm 139:17–18).

The hairs on your head may be enumerated, but God's thoughts towards you cannot be numbered. If you had access to them you could live out your whole lifetime enumerating them and never scratch the surface. The degree of God's concern is revealed in the multitude of His considerations. The omniscient One is thinking of you. (That, in and of itself, is a brain twister.) Because God loves you, He's thinking about you. Think about that.

If Father has carefully counted the hairs on your head, then surely you can count on this: there is nothing that concerns you which is insignificant to Him.

We have other examples in Scripture that tell of this personal love. John 3:16 speaks of God's love for the whole world, yet Scripture records that God Incarnate loved individuals: Lazarus and his family, the rich young ruler. Consider this: When Jesus washed the disciples' feet, He washed them one disciple at a time.

> Then He poured water into the basin, and began to wash the disciples' feet and to wipe them with the towel with which He was girded (John 13:5).

This was a personalized demonstration of Jesus' care for each of them. He was serving them. Even in a corporate setting, He washed one set of feet at a time.

Another testimony to the personal nature of God's love is found in John 17:23:

> I in them and You in Me, that they may be perfected in unity, so that the world may know that You sent Me, and loved them, even as You have loved Me.

We're loved "even as" Jesus was loved. Jesus was loved as an individual. So are we. The love God felt for Jesus, the love that Jesus experienced, was not vaguely ethereal. The Father's love was substantial. It was deeply personal devotion, care, affection, and delight. This is personal love. Please recall this: Jesus has commanded us to abide in this individualized love when He said, "Just as the Father has loved Me, so have I loved you; abide in My love" (John 15:9).

These various "witnesses" are communicating one thing about God's love: it is a personal love. God wants us to recognize the personal nature of His love. He wants us to welcome and embrace this love. He wants us to believe it. God wants us to grasp, not only "for God so loved the whole world," but particularly, "Who loved me and gave Himself up for me."

## God's Love is Greater

To enable us to understand God's true love we have stressed what we have in common with Him. Yet, there are some boundaries which must be faithfully addressed. Although our love is like His, and His love is like ours, there is a great difference between the quality and degree of our loves. He is the Creator; we are created.

For example, we think, and so does He. However, His thoughts are higher than ours in the same way the heavens are higher than the earth. It is the same with the power of His love. It is broader, longer, higher and deeper than ours.

To appreciate God's love you must be careful not to devalue His majesty or holiness. You can miss the blessing of knowing God's everlasting love if you depreciate the God who loves you.

Remember, your God is the blazing pure, only wise source of justice. Your God created and holds the universe together. It takes revelation to believe that He would pay any attention to you, let alone to believe that He loves you. Thank God, the revelation is available. It's in the Word, it's by the Spirit, it's in the community of believers.

The God of whom we are daring to write is the Creator of all things, seen and unseen. He is the God of Abraham, Isaac and Jacob. He is the Father of the Lord Jesus. He is all-powerful, all wise, and knows everything. God's love is filled with and energized by these attributes. He is transcendent, yet present with His creation everywhere all the time. He is totally virtuous. This is the One who really loves us with love that is true. He is revealed in His Son. His love is everlasting.

> I have loved you with an everlasting love (*agape*); therefore I have drawn you with lovingkindness (Jeremiah 31:3b).

## Chapter Summary

Our primary assertion in this chapter is that God's love is true love. It's not an imitation or just a love look-alike. God truly loves you! This love is deep and intense. It is emotional. It's based on "attraction." It is affectionate and paternal. And it is very personal. It is deeply interested, committed, and invested in *you*.

This is the quality of love which the Father, Son, and Spirit want to pour out upon you. Let faith in the objective evidence of the Word of God rise in your heart!

## Consider

*Jehovah Who Pines For You – Is God Wistful?*

Incredibly, the following verses describe someone who is heartbroken and longs for the past. God's unrequited love for Judah is revealed in the unhappy words of a frustrated lover.

> Can a virgin forget her ornaments, or a bride her attire? Yet My people have forgotten Me days without number (Jeremiah 2:32).

> Then the LORD said to me in the days of Josiah the king, "Have you seen what faithless Israel did? She went up on every high hill and under every green tree, and she was a harlot there. I thought, 'After she has done all these things she will return to Me'; but she did not return, and her treacherous sister Judah saw it" (Jeremiah 3:6–7).

*Adonai the Brokenhearted*

This next verse is very powerful. There is a word in Hebrew that testifies to God's heart being broken in pieces. If this wasn't in the Bible, I don't know that I would dare to make this statement.

> "Then those of you who escape will remember Me among the nations to which they will be carried captive, how I have been **hurt** [*broken in pieces, ruined*] by their adulterous hearts which turned away from Me, and by their eyes which played the harlot after their idols; and they will loathe themselves in their own sight for the evils which they have committed, for all their abominations" (Ezekiel 6:9).

We can relate to this type of experience. But what must it take for the Omnipotent One to experience heartbreak? What type of love is strong enough to break the heart of God?

1. What is the most important truth you learned in this chapter?

2. We have spoken about God's love being ardent, emotional, paternal, and devoted. Can you think of other aspects of God's love which the Scriptures attest to?

3.  Please read the following verse:

    > He tends his flock like a shepherd: He gathers the lambs in His
    > arms and carries them close to His heart; He gently leads those
    > that have young (Isaiah 40:11).

    This verse contains anthropomorphic language about God's
    heart towards Israel. Using the principle that God hears, only
    **more**, consider what this verse indicates about God's heart.
    Write out any insight you receive.

4.  Many individuals struggle with believing that God really, per-
    sonally loves them. Are there obstacles in your heart that
    prevent you from receiving God's personal love for you? De-
    scribe these obstacles. If you don't find obstacles in your own
    heart, write out an experience of receiving God's personal love.

5.  What did you struggle with the most in this chapter? Consider
    taking further time to study the Scriptures about this topic,
    and commit it to prayer.

6.  Please paraphrase, personalize and pray through Mark 10:21a:

    > Jesus looked at him and loved him.

# PART 3:

# RESTORING
# THE GOSPEL

*I don't know why Jesus loved me*
*I don't know why He cared*
*I don't know why He sacrificed His life*
*But I'm glad, so glad He did*

ANDRAE CROUCH

*Does he love us for his own sake, thus apparently jeopardizing the unselfish giving character of his love; or does he love us for our own sake, thus apparently jeopardizing his status as the highest value? The former would seem to compromise the love of God, the latter his glory. There is however, a third possibility. God loves us on the basis of that likeness of himself which he has placed within us, or in which he has created us.*

MILLARD J. ERICKSON

*God tells man who he is. God tells us that He created man in His image. So man is something wonderful.*

FRANCIS SCHAEFFER

*Essentially, what the OT says about man is determined by an encounter with and a relationship to God. That this God speaks and acts like a person brings about the living response and action of man....Man has a unique position among created beings.*

FRITZ MAAS, *Theological Dictionary of the Old Testament*

## Chapter 9

# What is Man?

*What is man that You take thought of him, and the son of man that You care for him? (Psalm 8:4).*

WE WANT TO DETERMINE WHY God loves humanity. In previous chapters we mentioned that we love what we find lovely (and so does God). So the first question we're going to ask is: Why is man lovely to God? There is a very simple answer for this question. Humanity is lovely to God because humanity was created to be the most lovely thing in Creation – the image of God. Let's develop this.

John tells us that our Creator "is love."

> The one who does not love does not know God, for God is love (1 John 4:8).

> And we have come to know and have believed the love which God has for us. God is love, and the one who abides in love abides in God, and God abides in him (1 John 4:16).

God's motivations are in accord with His nature. God is love, therefore, His motive in creation was love. One thing this indicates is that God purposed to create you so He may love you.

Through the Incarnation certain mysteries about God's nature have been more completely revealed. "No one has seen God at any time; the only begotten God who is in the bosom of the Father, He has explained Him" (John 1:18). The LORD, the Living God, is a Unity composed of three Persons with a defined order of relationship. He is Triune (Matthew 28:19). In His complete Self-awareness each Person of the Trinity is eternally, omnipotently, omnisciently interacting with free abandon and total commitment based upon *agape*. This love is demonstrated in Their zeal for the Other's glory (John 7:18; 12:28; 16:4; 17:5; Luke 12:10). In the Gospels we find the record of their mutual love. It was revealed through declaration and demonstration. Each member of the Trinity is appreciated and loved by the Others. God is holy (pure), gloriously beautiful, and He created you in His image and likeness. This was an act of love, with a motivation of love, for the purpose of love.

> Then God said, "Let Us make man in Our image, according to Our likeness; and let them rule over the fish of the sea and over the birds of the sky and over the cattle and over all the earth, and over every creeping thing that creeps on the earth." God created man in His own image, in the image of God He created him; male and female He created them. God blessed them; and God said to them, "Be fruitful and multiply, and fill the earth, and subdue it; and rule over the fish of the sea and over the birds of the sky and over every living thing that moves on the earth" (Genesis 1:26–28).

Our God is the extraordinarily skilled, omnipotent, all-wise Creator. He created us for a purpose – to be lovely to Him and to be loved by Him. By fashioning humanity in His image, God fulfilled this goal. We are successfully created to activate and attract His love. He created us to reveal and express attributes He especially cherishes about Himself.

The characteristics He loves are distilled, or crystallized, in humanity. They are not distorted or caricatured. Mankind has been designed to perfectly display these attributes. He perfectly recognizes these qualities in us. They couldn't be manifested any better than they are in humankind. Humanity is the essence of these attributes in the material dimension. God did not fail when He determined to perfectly fashion His image – He succeeded. And in achieving this goal of creating us in His image, He succeeded in creating humanity as something which is essentially lovely to Himself. You are lovely to God!

## God's Unique Image: Mankind

Psalm 19 and Romans 1 instruct us that inanimate and animate nature reveals the Glory and Power of the Godhead.

> The heavens are telling of the glory of God; and their expanse is declaring the work of His hands. Day to day pours forth speech, and night to night reveals knowledge (Psalm 19:1–2).

> For since the creation of the world His invisible attributes, His eternal power and divine nature, have been clearly seen, being understood through what has been made, so that they are without excuse (Romans 1:20).

Because nature itself reflects the Glory of God, even the "lesser qualities" which humanity shares with living and non-living creation reflect the image and Glory of God. For instance, at the most basic level, we share qualities with rocks. Rocks exist, and so do we. This reality images God's existence; He exists, so do we, and so do rocks.

> Now they may say to me, "What is His name?" What shall I say to them? God said to Moses, "I AM WHO I AM"; and He said, "Thus you shall say to the sons of Israel, 'I AM has sent me to you' " (Exodus 3:13b–14).

> The LORD is my rock (Psalm 18:2a).

Yet there is a major difference between us and rocks: humanity is the fullness of the image of God manifest in Creation.

Let's look at Genesis 1:26a:

> Then God said, "Let Us make man in Our image, according to Our likeness."

Unlike the rest of Creation, we have been uniquely created *b'tselem*: in (or *as*) the image of God. Representing God in both seen and unseen realms, humanity is the three-dimension image of God.

What is first revealed in Genesis is the Spirit of Elohim hovering over Creation. Then God spoke, and what He spoke came into existence. Imaging the activity of the Holy Spirit, humanity was created to work and cultivate the Garden (even as God cultivated Creation). Humanity's ability to subdue, control (in a limited way), and bring nature to fruition manifests the sovereignty of God.

The capacity to choose, or free will, especially when exercised for the good of others, is part of the image of God. Along with choice came the capacity to care for others, including things that are not immediate family or even of the same order. Human empathy so mirrors God that we are actually able to feel compassion for Creation. This is an example of the splendor of God's image. It is precious in His sight. He loves it when He sees it. Skill in acting in a loving manner reflects His glory as Creator.

Another thing we see in Genesis is Adam speaking to define and distinguish:

> Out of the ground the LORD God formed every beast of the field and every bird of the sky, and brought them to the man to see what he would call them; and whatever the man called a living creature, that was its name. The man gave names to all the cattle, and to the birds of the sky, and to every beast of the field, but for Adam there was not found a helper suitable for him (Genesis 2:19–20).

God named everything which He was about to create before He formed it. He said, "Let there be," and there was. Adam, as the head of humanity, reflected God as he named the creatures after their creation. Adam spoke from a place of comprehension – loving what God has made. Creation was made for us, as the objects of His love, in the same way He created us for Himself. As the head of humanity we find that Jesus is heir of the entire created order. This illustrates that Creation was made for humanity. This reality is reinforced through the revelation given to Paul; we are described as "fellow heirs with the Messiah" (Romans 8:17).

Humanity is created to reveal God to the Creation, as part of and in the midst of Creation. Mankind is to be the heart and hands and revelation of God to and in the midst of animate and inanimate nature. As God did this from heaven, so we were created to fulfill our role within the Garden of Eden (the garden of delight). As God is to all of which He is aware – so was humanity to nature. Even if nature doesn't understand our role, that also images God's action towards us. After all, we generally don't comprehend all God is doing either!

Along with the Creation account, other aspects of the image of God in humanity can be found in the Scriptures. Needless to say, we cannot exhaust the list here, but let's look at a few aspects of God's image in humanity.

## Relationships

We know through Scripture that God is a relational Being. We reflect God's image relationally. Within His relationships, God is just and loving. We are to relate to others as God would relate to them. He actively calls us to love and consequently pursue justice in our relationships. Our ability to do so images God.

> Be ye holy; for I am holy (1 Peter 1:16b).

God relates to humanity. Like God, we relate to other humans. God established humanity and social institutions.

> ...from whom every family in heaven and on earth derives its name (Ephesians 3:15).

> ...and He made from one man every nation of mankind to live on all the face of the earth, having determined their appointed times and the boundaries of their habitation (Acts 17:26).

Likewise, man is able to relate to others within the boundaries of what God has done and form societies, cultures, etc. Like God, we can establish friendships. Like God, we can relate to things lesser than mankind. Like God, we are able to relate to the spiritual realm. Like God, humanity is able to relate to God, Himself.

Let's expand. In the mystery of the Trinity we find that God has a relationship with and towards Himself. The following verses provide a glimpse of this:

> Then God said, "Let Us make man in Our image, according to Our likeness" (Genesis 1:26a).

> Then I heard the voice of the Lord, saying, "Whom shall I send, and who will go for Us?" Then I said, "Here am I. Send me!" (Isaiah 6:8).

> Come near to Me, listen to this: from the first I have not spoken in secret, from the time it took place, I was there. And now the Lord GOD has sent Me, and His Spirit (Isaiah 48:16).

> When He set for the sea its boundary so that the water would not transgress His command, when He marked out the foundations of the earth; then I was beside Him, as a master workman; and I was daily His delight, rejoicing always before Him, rejoicing in the world, His earth, and having my delight in the sons of men (Proverbs 8:29–31).

The members of the Trinity are working together, thinking together, sharing with One Another, and acting together to accomplish His ends. God relates to Himself. The Creator has determined that man image God in this aspect of His existence. He created humanity to relate to God!

> For now we see in a mirror dimly, but then face to face; now I know in part, but then I will know fully just as I also have been fully known (1 Corinthians 13:12).

Since we were created to know God, we image Him by having a relationship with Him that intrigues angelic majesties!

> It was revealed to them that they were not serving themselves, but you, in these things which now have been announced to you through those who preached the gospel to you by the Holy Spirit sent from heaven – things into which angels long to look (1 Peter 1:12).

Jesus has eternally been in relationship with the Father. As a man, He related to His Father similarly to how He related to God before the Incarnation. When the Holy Spirit has renewed the human spirit, humanity is able to function in direct relationship with the Godhead in aspects that image how God relates to Himself. This relationship is eternal life.

> This is eternal life, that they may know You, the only true God, and Jesus Christ whom You have sent (John 17:3).

> But the one who joins himself to the Lord is one spirit with Him (1 Corinthians 6:17).

Humanity also images God in the ability to know and share His mind and heart. Humanity can have faith in God's ability to accomplish His purposes. Humanity has the capacity to comprehend and love God in Spirit and in Truth. This is the essence of true worship, and an aspect of the image of God.

> But an hour is coming, and now is, when the true worshipers will worship the Father in spirit and truth; for such people the Father seeks to be His worshipers. God is Spirit, and those who worship Him must worship in spirit and truth (John 4:23–24).

## Communication

The capacity to communicate with language (which to some degree is shared with different animals) images God. Humanity is able to think before they speak and articulate for the purpose of inspiring others about the abstract (God, righteousness, reality or illusion, possibilities, plans, the past, etc.). Along with the ability to contemplate comes God's corresponding commandments to meditate, remember, celebrate and plan. The ability to think logically, to conclude in the abstract, to plan and accomplish what we have imagined, images God. Through communication History is preserved – and through that transmission we uniquely have a form of transgenerational memory. We can know and appreciate where we've come from and have hope for where we're going.

## Aesthetics

God gave humanity an appreciation for loveliness, pleasant sensations, beauty, and an ability to create correspondingly. God created the amazing beauty found in nature and then equipped us to appreciate along with Him that which He declared *good*. The Hebrew word *tov* communicates positive qualities ranging from beauty to moral excellence. In the same way He created, God gives us the ability to create aesthetically pleasing things. This aspect of His image is the motivation of creating in the arts. Every ethnic group seems to share the ability to compose songs, create music, fashion art, and tell stories. God even anoints the capacity to create beauty in certain people.

> Now the LORD spoke to Moses, saying, "See, I have called by name Bezalel, the son of Uri, the son of Hur, of the tribe of Judah. I have filled him with the Spirit of God in wisdom, in understanding, in knowledge, and in all kinds of craftsmanship" (Exodus 31:1–3).

Another aspect of creativity (closely related to communication) is found in imagining what does not yet exist, planning to make it and accomplishing our goals. Humanity can create practical things such as buildings and tools; our capacity to draw up blueprints, create, and manufacture new inventions images God.

Finally, let's consider this: we are able to enjoy visual wonders and recognize the Glory of God in Creation.

This appreciation is a clue to how He feels about you. We see the Glory of God in the beauty of Creation, and this ability images God. Yet, the Creator sees the pinnacle of the manifestation of His glory in Creation when He looks at you! To Him we are lovelier than the beauty of the rest of Creation. We are the image of God.

## Morality

Beyond instinct, there is another aspect of God's image which may be seen in a universal love of righteousness in humanity. Often this is culturally formed and can even be very warped, but it is still an aspect of the image of God which we are reflecting.

> For when Gentiles who do not have the Law do instinctively the things of the Law, these, not having the Law, are a law to themselves (Romans 2:14).

Any sense of appreciation for justice, mercy, and compassion, any ability to act in these ways, images God.

## Eternity

Part of the image of God is His eternal nature. We were created to exist forever. He couldn't create us to be transient beings; to image Him we had to be eternal. If we could be wiped out or annihilated we would not have been "as" His image. We would not have been a fit bride. Eternal life and eternal death are the consequences of being made to express the Glory of God.

## Dependence Upon God

Humanity images God when we are dependent only upon Him. God exists based upon nothing but Himself.

> God said to Moses, "I AM WHO I AM"; and He said, "Thus you shall say to the sons of Israel, 'I AM has sent me to you' " (Exodus 3:14).

> If I were hungry I would not tell you, for the world is Mine, and all it contains (Psalm 50:12).

We, also, are called to consciously exist with our foundation being in His Existence. Israel in the wilderness can be seen as a model of God's desired relationship with humanity (not in terms of obedience, but in terms of dependence). Another example of this is the Call of Abraham to leave the security of the known (his prior experience), and having left, to trust only in God. Ultimately this would lead to the call to sacrifice, not just his past, but His hopes for the future (Isaac)!

> He said, "Do not stretch out your hand against the lad, and do nothing to him; for now I know that you fear God, since you have not withheld your son, your only son, from Me" (Genesis 22:12).

Those who, as Abraham, walk by faith in the Lord's existence and nature mirror God's dependence upon nobody but Himself.

## Chapter Summary

The image of God is a wondrous thing because God Himself is wonderful: "How great is God – beyond our understanding!" (Job 36:26a). He is everything lovely, good, worthy, and beautiful. He created us in His image. God's image is lovely – the most lovely thing in created existence. We are lovely to God.

The mystery of God's love for us can be explained by His extraordinary creative ability: He made us to be lovely to Him, He made us to draw His love. The truth of this might cause us to gasp with incredulity. How was God able to do this? He succeeded in this goal because He is the Glorious Creator.

## Consider

> Then I was beside Him, as a master workman; and I was daily His
> delight, rejoicing always before Him, rejoicing in the world, His earth,
> and having my delight in the sons of men (Proverbs 8:30–31).

This is God's wisdom personified. What is Wisdom doing? Wisdom is seeing humanity and delighting in what is seen. God in His Wisdom delights in us. Apart from revelatory humility, we might think, "God, excuse me, but You have to be out of Your mind!" "No," He replies, "it's My Wisdom." What's being said in Proverbs 8 is that in the same way God delights in Wisdom, Wisdom is delighting in us.

Now, I would have no problem with this verse if it were referring to the Edenic state. "Yes, Lord, Your Wisdom rejoices in Adam. Adam is innocent. Adam is pure. Adam has not sinned." Yet, in this verse we read that the object of rejoicing is "in the sons of men." The Scripture doesn't record "sons of Adam" being born in the Garden. This is referring to the delight God's Wisdom receives as "she" interacts with fallen humanity – as fallen humanity receives "her" influence, "she" delights in them.

Now let's ask ourselves a couple of questions: Will we allow this word to affect us? Can we humble our perspectives and acquiesce to His joyous affection?

1.  What is the most important truth you learned in this chapter?

2.  Have you ever considered humanity as being lovely to God because they are the image of God? What does this mean about the pleasure God takes in humanity in the course of "normal life?" Think about ways you might be imaging God as you go through a normal day. What do you see there? How does God feel about His image in you at those times?

3.  Can you think of other aspects of the image of God in humanity which can be found in Scripture?

4.  Please read Psalm 149:4a:

    > For the LORD takes pleasure in His people.

    Have you ever clearly recognized the Lord taking pleasure in you? If so, describe that experience. If not, what do you think this experience would be like?

5.  What did you struggle with the most in this chapter? Consider taking further time to study the Scriptures about this topic, and commit it to prayer.

6.  Please paraphrase, personalize and pray through John 17:3:

    > This is eternal life, that they may know You, the only true God, and Jesus Christ whom You have sent.

*Amazing love! How can it be,*
*That Thou, my God, shouldst die for me?*

CHARLES WESLEY

*"We know that God so loved the world that He gave his only begotten Son. But wonder of wonders, WE are God's gift to God's Son!"*

EVAN WELSH

*In some way, it is natural for us to wish that God had designed for us a less glorious and less arduous destiny; but then we are wishing not for more love but for less.*

C. S. LEWIS

*God does not merely tolerate sinners: he loves them....God for all his ability to punish and for all his own spotless purity does not regard sinners with aversion, but with love, with the costly love that we see in the cross where Jesus died to save them.*

LEON MORRIS, *Dictionary of Jesus and the Gospels*

*Imagine coming across an abused Stradivarius...Now one person might think of this badly damaged instrument as a piece of junk and hardly give it notice. But another might look more closely and find the name of the master Antonio Stradivarius still legible on the broken instrument and recognize the worth of the damaged goods. At once his heart is broken that such an instrument could have been so abused; at the same time he makes plans to restore the instrument even if he must mortgage his home to do so. So it is with man. It is a mistake to regard even the most damaged of men as worthless...For man, fallen man, still bears the mark of his Maker.*

RONALD B. ALLEN, *The Majesty Of Man*

# Chapter 10

# Why is Man?

*For God so loved the world, that He gave His only begotten Son, that whoever believes in Him shall not perish, but have eternal life (John 3:16).*

WE HAVE ASKED AND FOUND AN ANSWER for the question, "Why does God love humanity?" Our next task is to answer this question: Why did God create man in the first place?

Sometimes to fully understand a person's reasons and actions we have to look to the end result. If you are a passenger in a car and the driver takes several unexpected turns, you might not know why until you see your destination. The reason for the activity – the motivation – is revealed by the outcome. In this case, the driver might have had a sudden craving for ice cream. Or perhaps they forgot something and are returning home to fetch it. The reason for their action is understood through the outcome of their activity.

When we look at the Scriptures, we find God doing some amazing things. There are some amazing "results" pointing at the reasons for His activity. For instance, let's consider the Exodus. Why did God deliver Israel? That's easy to answer, because we know the end of the story. He wanted to establish them as His own people in their own land, so they could worship and serve Him. What was God's motivation in doing that? Well, He desired them to be His own, He loved them, He wanted to do good to them. All of those purposes are borne out by His activity in the Exodus.

Looking at what the New Testament says about God's ultimate plans for the Church will reveal God's reasons in a similar manner. Think of some metaphors used to describe who and what the Church is supposed to be, or is, in God's eyes. Here are just a few: sons of God, heirs of God, friends of God, servants of God, co-laborers with God. Now, what does this tell us about why man is? Let's inquire a bit further based upon these descriptions: Who gets sons? Who gets friends? Who gets servants and co-laborers? God does! Take this further, who gets a bride? Who gets a body? Who gets a temple, a Kingdom of Priests? God does!

To understand why He created, perhaps we should ask: for whom did He create? God created for Himself, for the Trinity. In accordance with His nature of love, God created humanity as a "love-gift," to Himself.

We believe that God exists in Three Persons – Father, Son, and Spirit. This Trinity was in existence before Creation. They were always in eternal relationship. Before Creation, what was the relationship within the Godhead like? Was it competitive? Was there rivalry within the Godhead? Before the angels were made was the Son vying with the Father for worship?

We know through the Messiah's acts and words that the relationship within the Godhead is a loving relationship. This was true throughout eternity; God is love. What was true in the Incarnation was, is, and will be, true; there has always been loving interaction within the Godhead.

God's love is alive and relational. It is true that this love can exist in a state, but only if that state is dynamic. Before Creation there was an active love and communion within God Himself. Here's a descriptive hint of this relationship of God with Himself:

> In the beginning was the Word. The Word was with God. And the Word was God (John 1:1).

The Greek word for "with" ("the word was with God") is *pros*. It means towards, in relationship to, facing. "In the beginning was the Word…and the Word was *pros* God." This is not describing a static relationship. *Pros* describes a relationship where the pre-incarnate Messiah Jesus, being before God the Father forever, is delighting in His Father, moving into the infinite revelation of Who the Father is to the Son.

Jesus is towards His Father, and the Father is receiving His Son forever and forever and forever. This movement towards and into one another continues eternally. And the Spirit is rejoicing in Their midst. This glorious dynamic never has been, and never will be exhausted. God was not sad, bored or lonely. There was no necessity in Him to create anything to assuage any type of ache or longing.

## A Fresh Look at Creation

I envision Creation to be something like this:

In the midst of this eternal dynamo of love and joy between Father, Son, and Spirit, God the Father takes counsel within Himself saying, "Spirit, I want to somehow manifest My love for My Son. Let us make for Him a bride who will be able to love Him with the same loving comprehension of His glory with which I love Him. And not only that, through this bride My Son is going to know what it is like to be loved in the same way that I have been loved by Him."

> Let us rejoice and be glad and give the glory to Him, for the marriage of the Lamb has come and His bride has made herself ready (Revelation 19:7).

> He who has the bride is the bridegroom; but the friend of the bridegroom, who stands and hears him rejoices greatly because of the bridegroom's voice. So this joy of mine has been made full (John 3:29).

What kind of joy and satisfaction will Jesus receive on the day He marries His bride? This is an unsurpassed gift to Jesus — a love gift!

The Father wanted the Son to experience the love and joy which He, the Father, had received from the Son.

> This is My beloved Son, in whom I am well-pleased (Matthew 3:17b).

God the Father enjoyed *knowing* the Son's love. Because of His love for the Son, Father wanted His Son to experience the the same type of relationship. For this reason the bride was created. Father wants the bride to have the same love for the Son which He has. He places His perspective of the glory of Jesus in us. Abba releases His love for the Son through us. He created us to contain His love for the Son from a position of sonship. Thus the Son comes into the role and experience of fatherhood.

> For a child will be born to us, a son will be given to us...and His name will be called...Eternal Father (Isaiah 9:6).

> And again, "I will put my trust in Him." And again, "Behold, I and the children whom God has given me" (Hebrews 2:13).

Not only does Father enjoy the Son's love for Him, Abba thoroughly *enjoys* loving the Son. Loving the Son from the place of Fatherhood is a fantastic experience for God. He is well pleased in His Son. This is such a great experience that Abba wanted to give it away to His Son. Therefore the Father has taken great joy in exalting the Son. He loved the Son so much that He has given the Son the opportunity to enjoy loving in the same way Abba loves the Son. He so enjoyed loving the Son that as a gift He determined to create that which would give the pre-incarnate Son the same type of joy. Father planned to create that which would be so wonderful that the Son would have joyful love, just as He had joyful love in His Son. The Son would have somebody to love and enjoy just like the Father had joy in loving the Son.

Now reconsider Jesus' words: "Just as (*in the same way as*) the Father has loved Me so have I loved you; abide in My love." Father loved the Son with great joy, focus, delight, intensity, intimate comprehension, desire, openness, pleasure, and affirmation. "Just as the Father has loved Me..."

Let's move on and imagine the pre-Incarnate One saying to the Spirit, "Spirit, look at how My Father is rejoicing in the love which I am giving to Him! Let's make sons who can love Him with the same quality of love that I have for Him."

And the Spirit and the Son agree, "YES!"

> And I will be a father to you, and you shall be sons and daughters to Me," says the Lord Almighty (2 Corinthians 6:18).

Now at the same time, the Father and the Son look into One Another's heart and say, "Let's do something for the Spirit. Let's give Him a temple that won't constrain Him but which will free Him to be Himself, a place where He can find rest, a place where He can be at home. Let's make Him something that will further free Him just as He is free in Us. He has found such delight in Us and We have found such delight in Him, let us also give to Him that which can increase His joy. Let's create something *in* which He will be able to dwell, *with* which He will be able to fellowship, and *through* which He can move, just as He does in Us.

> Do you not know that you are a temple of God and that the Spirit of God dwells in you? (1 Corinthians 3:16).

## The Conclusion

"But where will We find something this wonderful? What shall We make? It's been six and a half days..." And They look at One Another and say:

Let Us make man in Our image, according to Our likeness
(Genesis 1:26).

Humanity was created as an amazing love gift to the Trinity!

# Examining the Metaphors of Redeemed Humanity

God uses metaphors to reveal hidden Spiritual realities. Just as anthropomorphic language conveys something true (only *more*), metaphors also reveal what is true. Consider these things: Hell is probably worse than fire! The Marriage Supper is certainly more than
just food. Yet, fire and food convey truth about hell and the heavenly state, respectively.

Let's look again at the "end" of humanity. What does God receive
as a result of creating us? According to Scripture, what are we to
God; how does He see us? What do these metaphors reveal to us?

## Through Creating Humanity the Father Receives Children

For all who are being led by the Spirit of God, these are sons of God.
For you have not received a spirit of slavery leading to fear again,
but you have received a spirit of adoption as sons by which we cry
out, "Abba! Father!" The Spirit Himself testifies with our spirit that
we are children of God, and if children, heirs also, heirs of God and
fellow heirs with Christ, if indeed we suffer with Him so that we may
also be glorified with Him (Romans 8:14–17).

See how great a love the Father has bestowed on us, that we would
be called children of God; and such we are. For this reason the world
does not know us, because it did not know Him. Beloved, now we
are children of God, and it has not appeared as yet what we will be.
We know that when He appears, we will be like Him, because we
will see Him just as He is (1 John 3:1–2).

## Father Receives a Kingdom of Priests

> ...and from Jesus Christ, the faithful witness, the firstborn of the dead, and the ruler of the kings of the earth. To Him who loves us and released us from our sins by His blood – and He has made us to be a kingdom, priests to His God and Father – to Him be the glory and the dominion forever and ever. Amen (Revelation 1:5–6).

## The Son Receives a Bride

The most intense human relationship is the most poignant mystery of our relationship with God. Yet it is merely a faint replica of what God has in store. More than any man can love a woman, more than any oneness that can be achieved; there is something astonishing in store for us as Jesus' bride!

> Husbands, love your wives, just as Christ also loved the church and gave Himself up for her, so that He might sanctify her, having cleansed her by the washing of water with the word, that He might present to Himself the church in all her glory, having no spot or wrinkle or any such thing; but that she would be holy and blameless. So husbands ought also to love their own wives as their own bodies. He who loves his own wife loves himself; for no one ever hated his own flesh, but nourishes and cherishes it, just as Christ also does the church, because we are members of His body. For this reason a man shall leave his father and mother and shall be joined to his wife, and the two shall become one flesh. This mystery is great; but I am speaking with reference to Christ and the church (Ephesians 5:25–32).

## The Son also Receives Brothers and Friends

> For those whom He foreknew, He also predestined to become conformed to the image of His Son, so that He would be the firstborn among many brethren (Romans 8:29).

> For both He who sanctifies and those who are sanctified are all from one Father; for which reason He is not ashamed to call them brethren,

saying, "I will proclaim Your name to my brethren, in the midst of the congregation I will sing Your praise" (Hebrews 2:11–12).

This is My commandment, that you love one another, just as I have loved you. Greater love has no one than this, that one lay down his life for his friends. You are My friends if you do what I command you (John 15:12–14).

## The Spirit Receives a Corporate Temple and Individual Temples

Or what agreement has the temple of God with idols? For we are the temple of the living God; just as God said, "I will dwell in them and walk among them; and I will be their God, and they shall be My people" (2 Corinthians 6:16).

Or do you not know that your body is a temple of the Holy Spirit who is in you, whom you have from God, and that you are not your own? (1 Corinthians 6:19).

## He Also Receives a Corporate Body and Individual Members

Now I rejoice in my sufferings for your sake, and in my flesh I do my share on behalf of His body, which is the church, in filling up what is lacking in Christ's afflictions (Colossians 1:24).

So we, who are many, are one body in Christ, and individually members one of another (Romans 12:5).

God said, "I am going to make them to be Your bride, to be Your sons, to be Your temple." Let me ask you another question: if you had the opportunity to choose the perfect life partner, would you select someone who would cause you to constantly grit your teeth and make a determined effort to love? Wouldn't you prefer someone that appealed to you in every way? Wouldn't you choose someone that was "ideal" for you? In creating His bride, is God less wise than you? Is He less passionate? Is He less practical?

No, He is more practical! In addition, He is the omnipotent, only-wise Creator, able to create the perfect bride for His Son. So, God, creating humanity to be His bride, made us in such a way that He would sincerely, really, eternally, willingly, fervently love us. He made us to be the most wonderful thing in the universe. He made us in His image. It was the most glorious thing He could do. His Son deserved nothing less.

Who God is, in Himself as Trinity, is the loveliest, holiest Being in existence. The image of God has been excellently fashioned to be the loveliest, holiest thing in Creation. How wonderful to be created for this purpose. How extraordinary it is to be created in God's image!

Not only is God's heart stirred by humanity, as if it was "love at first sight," but we have been created in such a way to enjoy being loved by Him for all of forever. Astonishingly, we have been created to thrill Him forever. We have been created and called to an eternally creative, stimulating, fascinating, holy relationship.

Apply the same "logic" to the metaphors of "temple," "body," "children." If you had unlimited resources, what type of house would you build for yourself? What type of body would you construct? What type of children? Would you love your ideal house? Your perfect body? Your beloved children? God created us to be the objects of this type of love as a gift to Himself. God created you to be so special that He could demonstrate His love for the Son by giving you to Jesus!

God shall accomplish all He purposes concerning humanity. It shall be echoed in heaven:

> O Lord GOD, Thou hast begun to show Thy servant Thy greatness and Thy strong hand; for what god is there in heaven or on earth who can do such works and mighty acts as Thine? (Deuteronomy 3:24).

In every way, God made man as the ideal bride, friends, sons, priests, brothers, temple, body for Himself. We were created to be uniquely beautiful and satisfying to God.

## Our Current Condition

As we saw in the last chapter, the mystery of God's love for all humanity is solved in the glory of His creative ability. He succeeded in creating humanity for the purpose of attracting – drawing – His love. That includes you. Yet, considering the current condition of humanity, is fallen man still lovely?

> To the woman He said, "I will greatly multiply Your pain in childbirth, in pain you will bring forth children; yet your desire will be for your husband, and he will rule over you." Then to Adam He said, "Because you have listened to the voice of your wife, and have eaten from the tree about which I commanded you, saying, 'You shall not eat from it;' cursed is the ground because of you; in toil you will eat of it all the days of your life. Both thorns and thistles it shall grow for you; and you will eat the plants of the field; by the sweat of your face you will eat bread, till you return to the ground, because from it you were taken; for you are dust, and to dust you shall return" (Genesis 3:16–19).

Even after the Fall, humanity remains His image. In fact, even within the Curse found in Genesis 3:16–19, man continues to image God. Man's pain images God's new relationship with humanity and the Creation. Man is God's Eden which is now bringing forth thorns and thistles. As childbearing is done in pain, so through Jesus' suffering God brought forth the rebirth. There is tension between man and woman as between God and humanity.

The Bible is not romantic about man's nature. Look at these two Scriptures:

> The heart is more deceitful than all else and is desperately sick; who can understand it? (Jeremiah 17:9).

As it is written, "There is none righteous, not even one; there is none who understands, there is none who seeks for God; all have turned aside, together they have become useless; there is none who does good, there is not even one" (Romans 3:10–12).

But man is still the image of God. Here are two witnesses to this in Scripture:

Whoever sheds man's blood, by man his blood shall be shed, for in the image of God He made man (Genesis 9:6).

With it we bless our Lord and Father, and with it we curse men, who have been made in the likeness of God (James 3:9).

No doubt we are a somewhat distorted image because of a wrong focus and foundation; perhaps one could even say we are a perverted image. Yet humanity still manifests God to Creation. According to the Scriptures, we haven't ceased to be lovely to God. We are, tragically, beloved by Him. We are taking the treasure we are and wasting it on vanity and evil.

## God's Bride

Let's look again at the metaphors of who, or what, we are to God. In the foundational metaphor of the bride, we have not ceased to be lovely to Him. We have become adulterous – like Gomer, like Judah.

When the LORD first spoke through Hosea, the LORD said to Hosea, "Go, take to yourself a wife of harlotry and have children of harlotry; for the land commits flagrant harlotry, forsaking the LORD" (Hosea 1:2).

Then the LORD said to me, "Go again, love a woman who is loved by her husband, yet an adulteress, even as the LORD loves the sons of Israel, though they turn to other gods and love raisin cakes" (Hosea 3:1).

"How languishing is your heart," declares the Lord GOD, "while you do all these things, the actions of a bold-faced harlot" (Ezekiel 16:30).

To further understand this, try to identify with a time when your heart was broken. Were you ever rejected by someone you loved? Did they immediately cease to be lovely? The people I know who have had their spouses desert them for someone else suffered deep heartbreak and excruciating jealousy. Think about this: the unfaithful partner did not cease to be lovely, they were still desirable, but in the eyes of the spurned spouse the adulterer was in love with the wrong person! In the same way, God still loves unfaithful humanity.

For while we were still helpless, at the right time Christ died for the ungodly. For one will hardly die for a righteous man; though perhaps for the good man someone would dare even to die. But God demonstrates His own love toward us, in that while we were yet sinners, Christ died for us (Romans 5:6–8).

## God's Children

In the foundational metaphor of Children, we have not ceased to be beloved. We have become rebels and hateful – like Absalom, or the Prodigal. Rebellious humanity is breaking the heart of God. Prodigal humanity is maddeningly frustrating the Father.

In this manner Absalom dealt with all Israel who came to the king for judgment; so Absalom stole away the hearts of the men of Israel (2 Samuel 15:6).

Listen, O heavens, and hear, O earth; for the LORD speaks, "Sons I have reared and brought up, but they have revolted against Me. An ox knows its owner, and a donkey its master's manger, but Israel does not know, My people do not understand." Alas, sinful nation, people weighed down with iniquity, offspring of evildoers, sons who act corruptly! They have abandoned the LORD, they have despised the Holy One of Israel, they have turned away from Him (Isaiah 1:2–4).

The younger of them said to his father, "Father, give me the share of the estate that falls to me." So he divided his wealth between them.

And not many days later, the younger son gathered everything to-gether and went on a journey into a distant country, and there he squandered his estate with loose living. Now when he had spent everything, a severe famine occurred in that country, and he began to be impoverished (Luke 15:12–14).

## God's House

In the foundational metaphor of the Temple, we have not ceased to be desirous as a dwelling place. We have become a house of idolatrous filth – like Manasseh, like a den of thieves. This is God's house! It was made according to His specifications. He loved dwelling there and now He's exiled from His own home through no fault of His own.

He made his son pass through the fire, practiced witchcraft and used divination, and dealt with mediums and spiritists. He did much evil in the sight of the LORD provoking Him to anger. Then he set the carved image of Asherah that he had made, in the house of which the LORD said to David and to his son Solomon, "In this house and in Jerusalem, which I have chosen from all the tribes of Israel, I will put My name forever" (2 Kings 21:6–7).

And He found in the temple those who were selling oxen and sheep and doves, and the money changers seated at their tables. And He made a scourge of cords, and drove them all out of the temple, with the sheep and the oxen; and He poured out the coins of the money changers and overturned their tables; and to those who were selling the doves He said, "Take these things away; stop making My Father's house a place of business" (John 2:14–16).

## His Response

What is God's response to all of this? Does He just write us off as a bad investment of Holy Wise Omnipotence? No! The Living God longs for restoration of His marriage. He is heartbroken over and longs for the return of His child. He is zealous for the cleansing of His house! The Warrior God really loves us and has determined – He has *determined* – to bring us back to Himself.

It is within this context that we should read the capstone of revelation about God's motivation in redemption.

> For God so loved the world, that He gave His only begotten Son, that whoever believes in Him shall not perish, but have eternal life (John 3:16).

To further understand our value to God, let's read some of Jesus' parables with a fresh perspective.

## Parables of Love and Desire: Understanding Our Value

Jesus used many parables to express God's love and desire for humanity. Consider these stories again through the lens of humanity being a love gift for God.

> The kingdom of heaven is like a treasure hidden in the field, which a man found and hid again; and from joy over it he goes and sells all that he has and buys that field. Again, the kingdom of heaven is like a merchant seeking fine pearls, and upon finding one pearl of great value, he went and sold all that he had and bought it (Matthew 13:44–46).

To God, we are "the pearl of great price." Seeing the pearl (humanity) lying forgotten in a field (the cosmos) He sold all that He had to bankroll Himself (gave His Son) to buy the field (redeem us) to gain the pearl (humanity)!

The only wise God is the final arbiter of reality. He alone is able to discern the true worth of anything. We are given this parable that we may understand our true value and the extent of God's love. In God's sight we are worth everything at His disposal. The holy mystery is that this included His Son Who was given on our behalf.

In Luke 15 the Messiah gave three parables to answer those who criticized the way He received sinners. Evidently, they felt that sinners were despised, dismissed by God as unclean, and that therefore they should be rejected by those who were righteous.

First Jesus gave the parable of the lost sheep, then the lost coin, and finally, the lost son. In each case the shepherd, the housewife, and the father call for a party to celebrate the recovery of that which had been lost. At the end of the first two parables, the Lord Jesus told us that there is joy in heaven amongst heaven's angels when a sinner repents. He illustrates this joy in the parable of the Lost Son when the father decrees a feast to celebrate the son's return. Look, the angels don't rejoice without cause; there is joy in heaven because Father has called for a party!

Rather than abhorring and rejecting sinners, God the Father is avidly searching for them. God's love is immutable (unchangingly consistent) in its focus. He loves you now the same way He loved you when He redeemed you. Remember the parable of the Prodigal Son. We can dare to say that His love is "now" love: it is love that is searching for you *now*, His heart is reaching out to you *now*, He wants His love to be known now. Father waits for us to look to Him so He may reveal His love to us *now*. Right now, no matter what you have done, no matter how far you have strayed, you can look to God and begin to experience His *now* love!

According to these parables, sinners do not cease to be lovely to God. God's love is unwaveringly directed at you. At this moment, His love is searching for and desiring every person that He has made.

## Review

God created man to be lovely to Himself; God fashioned us as a love-gift for Himself. We are ideally made to suit God. Though we are fallen, we are still lovely to God. His love is immutable; we don't cease to be lovely because we are fallen. Rather, His broken and desirous heart keeps yearning; His jealous love is searching. Through the work of Messiah at the Cross God is determinedly drawing us, calling and making a way for us to return to Himself.

## Reexamining John 3:16

We are going to end this chapter by taking a fresh look at John 3:16. This simple verse contains the simple Gospel. In it is powerful revelation about God's motivation towards humanity. Yet, perhaps because of its familiarity, we've replaced God's motivation (which is love) with our own thoughts about His motivations. The verse reads like this:

> For God so loved the world that He gave His one and only Son that whoever believes in Him shall never perish but have eternal life.

Although this is easy to read and easy to understand, people often subconsciously substitute different meanings than what has been plainly written. Consider eight alternative sayings John could have written to reveal a different *purpose* than *agape*:

1. God did not send His son into the world because of a hunger for worship. It was not just for His **praise**...

   > For God so **desired the glory due His name** that He created some people to stand around His throne to praise Him. They fell, and God wanted to redeem them to fulfill His original purpose. So, He gave His one and only Son so that whoever believes in Him shall never perish but instead will praise Him forever.

2. Furthermore, God was not looking for the right moment to demonstrate His Sovereignty. John 3:16 does not reveal the motive of God seeking to exercise His **preference**. This verse doesn't read like this:

   > For God desired to reveal His sovereignty, so even though He disliked the world, He gave His one and only Son and **picked**

people (according to His inexplicable preference) to believe in Him. These picked people shall never perish but demonstrate His sovereignty forever.

3. Neither did He send His only begotten Son because He valued our **potential**. John 3:16 does not read like this:

> For God so **valued the potential** of a redeemed humanity that He gritted His teeth, strengthened His will, and gave His one and only Son for people He really didn't like, so that whoever believes in Him shall never perish but fulfill their potential, eventually being conformed to the image of the Son of God so they might finally be worth loving.

4. It was not merely a matter of God being moved to **pity** our state and destiny.

> For God so **pitied** a lost and fallen humanity that was heading for, and deserved, eternal conscious torment in hell that He gave His one and only Son, because He is a compassionate Person, so that whoever believes in Him shall never perish but have eternal life.

5. Neither did God give His Son to be crucified to **put things right**.

> For God so desired to **put things right** that He gave His only Son to banish moral and spiritual evil from the created order, and by the way, if you believe this includes your sin and fallen nature, you'll have everlasting life.

6. Nor was He motivated to redeem us that He might exert His **power** and **authority** through us.

> For God so desired to **exercise His power** and **authority** over the devil, through redeemed humanity, that He gave His one and only Son so that whoever believes in Him shall never perish but release and exercise God's government over all Creation.

7. Jesus was not sent so we may be **perfected**.

> For God so desired to **transform humanity** into the image of His Son that He gave His one and only Son so that whoever believes

in Him shall never perish but be revealed as the glorified children of God, displaying His attributes to an admiring and sub-
servient Creation forever.

8.   Neither did He send His Son because He is **perfectly wonderful**.
John 3:16 does not say the following:

For God was such a **perfectly wonderful** Person that He gave
His only Son so that whoever believes in Him shall never perish
but have eternal life.

Now, the Scriptures reveal that we do have incredible potential. We
also know that God is incredibly and perfectly wonderful and worthy of our praise. God shall transform us. We shall rule with Him.
But this is not *why* Father sent His Son. The Father, this wonderfully wonderful Person, *loves us*. Our God has come to redeem us.
He is bringing us back to Himself.

This is what the verse says:

For God so *loved* the world that He gave His one and only Son so that
whoever believes in Him shall never perish but have eternal life.

Recognizing God's incredible love for humanity, our current role
and future destiny as His friends, bride, temple, sons, and our incredible design in His image restores the Gospel that is clearly pro-
claimed in John 3:16. For love…He did it for love. He did it for us.
This is the Gospel of Jesus the Messiah.

## Chapter Summary

God created man to be lovely to Himself. We are the image of
God. We have been wonderfully fashioned so we would spark and
draw God's love. God created us as a precious love-gift for Himself. We are ideally made to suit God. Though we are fallen, we are
still lovely to God. We don't cease to be lovely because we are fallen.
Rather, His broken, jealous, desirous heart keeps yearning…calling.
God has made a way for us to return. Through what God has done

at Calvary He will ultimately get His heart's desire. His love for us is rooted in Creation and realized through Redemption.

> I have wiped out your transgressions like a thick cloud and your sins like a heavy mist. Return to Me, for I have redeemed you (Isaiah 44:2).

> But the LORD was pleased to crush Him, putting Him to grief; if He would render Himself as a guilt offering, He will see His offspring, He will prolong His days, and the good pleasure of the LORD will prosper in His hand. As a result of the anguish of His soul, He will see it and be satisfied; by His knowledge the Righteous One, My Servant, will justify the many, as He will bear their iniquities (Isaiah 53:10–11).

> And Jesus answered them, saying, "The hour has come for the Son of Man to be glorified. Truly, truly, I say to you, unless a grain of wheat falls into the earth and dies, it remains alone; but if it dies, it bears much fruit" (John 12:23–24).

God wants you to know this love.

## Consider

The Messiah spoke of God's determination to restore fallen humanity to Himself:

> You gave Him authority over all flesh, that to all whom You have given Him, He may give eternal life. This is eternal life, that they may know You, the only true God, and Jesus Christ whom You have sent (John 17:2–3).

He is actively working towards this goal. Part of His labor towards this end is accomplished through our participation with Him. As we comprehend the love of this brokenhearted Warrior God, we will desire to reciprocate. We reciprocate by embracing His heart and His mission as our own. Humanity will become precious to us because they are precious to the One we love.

He is looking for those who will allow His love to work in them, to release the fullness of His love to those who are lost. Through His activity and our own cooperation with Messiah, His redemptive work through Jesus will bear the fruit He desires. His wife returns, His children come home, His home is cleansed and ready for Him to dwell. You can enter in. Begin by embracing His love for the lost. Begin to recognize the heartbroken love of God. You will want to join Him in bringing humanity home.

1.  What is the most important truth you learned in this chapter?

2.  Take one of these metaphors about humanity's destiny: Body, Friends, Kingdom of Priests, and apply the concept of God ideally forming us to be suited to Himself. What does it mean that we are God's ideal Body, God's ideal Friends, God's ideal Kingdom of Priests?

3.  Please read Romans 15:30:

    > Now I urge you, brethren, by our Lord Jesus Christ and by the love of the Spirit, to strive together with me in your prayers to God for me.

    In this verse the love of the Holy Spirit is explicitly mentioned. At times, it is easy to neglect the importance and role of this third Person of the Trinity. In your opinion, what does it mean that the Holy Spirit loves you? What is it like to be loved by the Spirit of God?

4.  The concept of being created as a love gift for the Trinity is an immense idea. Setting aside issues like our sin, fallen nature, and inability to appropriately respond, describe how you think God feels about this love gift for Himself.

5.  Another way we image God is when we offer ourselves to the Lord as a love-gift. This act is described in Romans 12:1:

> Therefore I urge you, brethren, by the mercies of God, to present your bodies a living and holy sacrifice, acceptable to God, which is your spiritual service of worship.

How do you think the Lord feels about this?

6. What did you struggle with the most in this chapter? Consider taking further time to study the Scriptures about this topic, and commit it to prayer.

7. Please paraphrase, personalize and pray through John 3:16:

> For God so loved the world, that He gave His only begotten Son, that whoever believes in Him shall not perish, but have eternal life.

# PART 4:

# PURSUING

*Batter my heart, three-person'd God; for you*
*As yet but knock; breathe, shine, and seek to mend;*
*That I may rise, and stand, o'erthrow me, and bend*
*Your force, to break, blow, burn, and make me new.*
*I, like an usurp'd town, to another due,*
*Labour to admit you, but O, to no end.*
*Reason, your viceroy in me, me should defend,*
*But is captived, and proves weak or untrue.*
*Yet dearly I love you, and would be loved fain,*
*But am betroth'd unto your enemy;*
*Divorce me, untie, or break that knot again,*
*Take me to you, imprison me, for I,*
*Except you enthrall me, never shall be free,*
*Nor ever chaste, except you ravish me.*

JOHN DONNE

*Measure not God's love and favour by your own feeling.*
*The sun shines as clearly in the darkest day as it does in the brightest.*
*The difference is not in the sun, but in some clouds which hinder*
*the manifestation of the light thereof.*

RICHARD SIBBES

*It is hard for a sinful man to believe that God loves Him. His own accusing*
*conscience tells him it could not be so. He knows that he is an enemy of God*
*and alienated in his mind through wicked works, and he sees in himself a*
*thousand moral discrepancies that unfit him for the just enjoyment of so*
*pure a love. Yet the whole Bible proclaims the love of God for sinful men.*
*We must believe in His love because He declares it and avail ourselves of the*
*sanctifying grace of Christ in order to receive and enjoy that love to the full.*

A. W. TOZER

## Chapter 11

# Overcoming Obstacles

*The LORD is close to the brokenhearted and saves those who are crushed in spirit (Psalm 34:18).*

WE HAVE ALMOST COME TO THE END of our introductory examination of God's love (though we've scarcely scratched the surface of this topic). There is so much more that could be said. Yet we trust that this study has given you fuel for a fresh start in seeking to know the love of God. From this foundation, you can build and be built. Before we close, I want to provide you with some practical help for pursuing the knowledge of God's love. I also want to help those who might say, "I really want this, but I can't seem to break through into receiving this love."

Because the New Testament reveals that knowing God's love is normative for every believer, let's start by recognizing and confessing: "This is for me!" Let faith arise in your heart based on the Word of God upon which you've been meditating throughout these chapters. From that point, you can take the following information and begin pressing in to apprehend and receive this love that is "yours."

### Obstacles

There are obstacles to fully adjusting ourselves to this message of the love of God. One reason Jesus instructed us to pray that Father's

Kingdom would come and that His will would be done is because the Kingdom is contested in this fallen world. We're going to look at a few of the most common hindrances you might already be encountering as you seek to come to terms with these truths.

## The Enemy

There is an adversary who will seek to prevent you from grasping the love of God. From the beginning he impugned God's goodness:

> The serpent said to the woman, "You surely will not die! For God knows that in the day you eat from it your eyes will be opened, and you will be like God, knowing good and evil" (Genesis 3:4–5).

He still seeks to make God's goodness, His love, look like something other than what it is. The devil desires to bind us and blind us to the wonderful news which leads to a righteous, trusting, intimate relationship with God. Satan wants us bowed down, in bondage to him. He seeks to steal the Word of God.

> Now the parable is this: the seed is the word of God. Those beside the road are those who have heard; then the devil comes and takes away the word from their heart, so that they will not believe and be saved (Luke 8:11–12).

This word of God's love for you is going to be contested. Generally speaking, the more important the teaching, the more bitterly it is resisted. This message is important and it's going to be opposed. The adversary is going to dispute the Word. We must be determined to stand our ground and believe what we find written in Scripture.

> But the seed in the good soil, these are the ones who have heard the word in an honest and good heart, and hold it fast, and bear fruit with perseverance (Luke 8:15).

Guard this message. Don't allow the adversary to rob you. Jesus said that there would be hearers who have honest and good hearts.

Why can't that be you? Review what you've studied. Share the truths you've learned. Speak to God about His love and ask Him to confirm it. Guard the word like a treasure; don't let it get away; "Hold it fast." Act in faith upon the basis of the truth of His love for you. Persevere.

## Wrong Teaching

One scheme the enemy has employed (2 Corinthians 2:11) is the dissemination of a distorted definition of *agape*. The devil has been maliciously perverting truth from the very beginning (Genesis 3:4–5). It is sad that many of the teachers in the Church have been taken off track on this important topic. Misinformation and wrong emphases about His love are common, and most people are not focused upon it at all. Some even believe that focusing on the love of God will derail you from fruitful service. How wrong this mindset is!

Without really holding on to God's Word, and choosing to base your understanding and practice upon that Word, it can be easy to lose any ground taken through this study. We must be like the Bereans:

> For they received the word with great eagerness, examining the Scriptures daily to see whether these things were so (Acts 17:11b).

This is a call to begin to follow through by enthusiastically pursuing the truth of what you've received. Examine the Scriptures about God's love. Let the Word, not the teachings of men, nor the experience of others, dictate what you believe about the love of God. Actively hold on to the understanding you have gained. Stay in the Scriptures, weigh things against the Word. "Receive the word implanted" (James 1:21).

It is important to note that all of us are called to instruct others. We "ought to be teachers" (Hebrews 5:12b). Yet, God has also given seasoned, gifted teachers to the Church (Ephesians 4:11). Every one of us shall give an account to God for the careless words we've spoken (Matthew 12:36). In the light of this, here are exhortations to every believer, and especially to those specifically called to minister the Word (Acts 6:4). These apostolic encouragements are pertinent to this topic:

> Retain the standard of sound words which you have heard from me, in the faith and love which are in Christ Jesus. Guard, through the Holy Spirit who dwells in us, the treasure which has been entrusted to you (2 Timothy 1:13–14).

> Be diligent to present yourself approved to God as a workman who does not need to be ashamed, accurately handling the word of truth (2 Timothy 2:15).

Of course, any aspect of truth about God's love can strengthen the believing community. Even sub-Biblical definitions have brought forth a dynamic and relevant witness to the reality of the Kingdom. Also, the holy experiences the Spirit conveys to our hearts are not dependent upon "right understanding" or "right interpretation." However, I remember the moment I saw that false definitions of love were masquerading as a superior form of love to the *agape* the Bible ascribes to God. I discerned that these teachings are actually strongholds. These strongholds exalt themselves over and against the knowledge of God. If the truth is intended to set us free, if God wants us to know Him upon the basis of His love, what better strategy than to distort the meaning of the word *agape* itself? Please be encouraged to review the teaching you've received in this book. Read and pray. Cast down inadequate teachings and establish the truth. Teach others the truth. Experience the truth with others.

> For the weapons of our warfare are not of the flesh, but divinely powerful for the destruction of fortresses. We are destroying speculations and every lofty thing raised up against the knowledge of God, and we are taking every thought captive to the obedience of Christ (2 Corinthians 10:4–5).

## Ourselves

The primary hindrance to obtaining a personal knowledge of the love of God comes from within us.

> The heart is more deceitful than all else and is desperately sick; who can understand it? (Jeremiah 17:9).

Fundamentally, apart from God *we are unable* to grasp His love. We all tend towards legalism, laziness, skepticism, and sin. If we depend upon ourselves, we will fail to prioritize the knowledge of God's love.

Let's return to the parable of the Kingdom known as the Parable of the Sower. As we read those sacred words we are reminded that the devil is not the only reason the Word doesn't change our lives. There are two other explanations the Messiah reveals. Those reasons have to do with the state of our hearts.

> Those on the rocky soil are those who, when they hear, receive the word with joy; and these have no firm root; they believe for a while, and in time of temptation fall away. The seed which fell among the thorns, these are the ones who have heard, and as they go on their way they are choked with worries and riches and pleasures of this life, and bring no fruit to maturity (Luke 8:13–14).

Our own hearts make it difficult to apprehend this love. We must make a decision and then with determination press into God for grace and revelation. Through the work of the cross and resurrection of the Messiah, there is an overflow of enabling favor available to us. In fact, there is "grace for grace" (John 1:16b) being given to us right now. God desires to give us the "power to grasp" (Ephesians 3:18). He fills the "hungry with good things" (Luke 1:53a).

## Condemnation

Our actions and attitudes often show a self-centered lack of love. As His image we are called to reveal the full glory of His nature, yet we fall short of the actions and attitudes we know God wants us to have (Romans 3:23). Sometimes we willfully turn from Him. This provides ground for subconscious condemnation. If that is your condition, consciously come as a Prodigal Son. Your Father awaits your return. If you have sinned, but then turned to God for cleansing, Father is willing to reaffirm His love for you. Read 2 Corinthians 2:8:

> I urge you, therefore, to reaffirm your love for him.

In the same way the Church is encouraged to reaffirm its *agape* for a returning sinner, so your Father receives and reaffirms you, only **more**! The parable of the Prodigal Son has been given to you that you may be assured of the type of reception God will give to you.

> And he got up and came to his father. But while he was still a long way off, his father saw him, and felt compassion for him, and ran and embraced him, and kissed him (Luke 15:20).

The people in Jesus' parables are always "earthy." I've heard an unlikely tale of a saintly father, anxiously peering out the front bay window of his split-level too many times. I doubt it. I bet that many a night around the table the father and older brother spoke at length about what the prodigal deserved. How they would treat *him* if he ever came back! How they would make him *pay*! More times than would be charitable to guess, the father probably felt like breaking the younger son's neck – just like that son had broken his heart.

Yet, one day as he was getting ready to oversee his fields he happened to glance down the road. He saw an all too familiar, though tired, gait. The father couldn't help himself. A reflexive churning of his gut caught him off guard. A visceral compassion – practically biological in nature – welled up and sent him bolting down the path to see his emaciated son face to face.

Even while he was stumbling over himself in haste, there was a part of this dad's mind that couldn't believe he was actually running toward the youth. His soul was churning out prearranged plans to repay that traitor – to reproach the ingrate. Panting from the exertion, running to his son, compassion betrayed his mind – tears coursed down his cheeks. Ready to caustically reprove him with long rehearsed sarcasm, his heart overcame his resentful pride. He found himself embracing his child, compulsively kissing him – betraying his better judgment, embarrassing himself, and totally undoing the son.

Most of us read the story of the prodigal son as if the father is ideal, a perfect reflection of the Father in heaven. However, think of the unjust judge, the conniving pearl merchant, the unrighteous steward, the woman searching for her silver, and other unaffected, natural players in the King's parables. These characters are far from perfect. The question that should occur to us in reading the story of the Prodigal Son is this: "If a wounded, bitter father would so receive his treacherous, narcissistic offspring, how much more will your heavenly Father receive you?"

Where is the reproach? Where the condemnation? Where is the recriminating, "I told you so"?

Notice Abba's reaction portrayed in parable form. The father of the prodigal saw his son's state. What he saw moved him to compassion. Compassion moved the father – who ran towards, embraced, and kissed the child who had betrayed his heart.

But what about the circumstances of the backslider? The prodigal had totally blown his inheritance. He had forfeited the respect of everyone in the household. The only right thing he did was repent – and even that was not from the best of motives.

Not only was the child personally received, he was positionally restored!

> But the father said to his slaves, "Quickly bring out the best robe and put it on him, and put a ring on his hand and sandals on his feet; and bring the fattened calf, kill it, and let us eat and be merry; for this son of mine was dead, and has come to life again; he was lost, and has been found." And they began to be merry (Luke 15:22–24).

> Jesus asked, "If you then, being evil, know how to give good gifts to your children, how much more shall your Father who is in heaven give what is good to those who ask Him!" (Matthew 7:11).

Look how this pathetically human father received his devious son. How much more graciously will your Father in heaven receive you? This is the story of our Father's life. This may be your story, too.

> "Let the wicked forsake his way and the unrighteous man his thoughts; and let him return to the LORD, and He will have compassion on him, and to our God, for He will abundantly pardon. For My thoughts are not your thoughts, neither are your ways My ways," declares the LORD. "For as the heavens are higher than the earth, so are My ways higher than your ways, and My thoughts than your thoughts" (Isaiah 55:7–9).

I want to encourage you to consider "how much more…your Father" will receive you. If you are struggling with condemnation because of unloving actions, imperfect consecration, or outright rebellion, do not allow that to keep you from returning to the Lord. Your God will run to you.

## Rejection and Other Emotional Bondage

Along with condemnation, people might have a whole host of feelings and thoughts about who God is that might keep them from coming to Him. It's amazing what lies we can believe about Him when the Word so clearly testifies to His character and nature. How many believers think they are some special case to whom the good news of God's love does not apply? Rejection and emotional bondage are real hindrances to fellowship with the loving heart of God.

Let's look again at the Prodigal Son. If God will receive sinners in such a way, how do you think He receives those who are seeking to serve Him, who are desperate to please Him? Who are truly grieved over their rebellion? Is He a less loving Father to those experiencing different troubles? How does God respond to broken people?

Look at what Jesus said: "He has sent me to bind up the brokenhearted" (Luke 4:18). Does this sound like someone Who will reject you? He has been sent to find you! He is searching for you (Luke 15:4,8; 19:20). When you come in your brokenness, do you think He will turn you away? Let's look to the testimony of Scripture:

> The Spirit of the Lord GOD is upon me, because the LORD has anointed me to bring good news to the afflicted; He has sent me to bind up the brokenhearted, to proclaim liberty to captives and freedom to prisoners (Isaiah 61:1).

> The LORD is close to the brokenhearted and saves those who are crushed in spirit (Psalm 34:18).

> He heals the brokenhearted and binds up their wounds (Psalm 147:3).

> "For My hand made all these things, thus all these things came into being," declares the LORD. "But to this one I will look, to him who is humble and contrite of spirit, and who trembles at My word" (Isaiah 66:2).

> The sacrifices of God are a broken spirit; a broken and a contrite heart, O God, You will not despise (Psalm 51:17).

> The one who comes to Me I will certainly not cast out (John 6:37b).

Sometimes those who sought to find fault with the Messiah were insightful. For instance, in Luke 15:2b we find the record of this accusation, "This man receives sinners and eats with them." Jesus did not argue with them. In fact, we find that even after His ascension the exalted King implores an outrageously backslidden church to open up to Him so He might share a meal with them (Revelation 3:20). Jesus has not changed.

To receive the love of God, you can reorient your mind and begin to exalt the Scriptures above your experiences, problems, and fears. This testimony of the love of God is true. He has demonstrated the degree of His devotion. The good news of His reception for broken individuals is true. Choose to place trust in this report, and, if faith is difficult, then at least let hope arise in your heart.

Rather than remaining imprisoned in a place of brokenness and unbelief, begin to ask Him to set you free. Begin to believe that the One Who can regenerate the worst of sinners can restore you to spiritual health. Take some of the key Scriptures in this book and commit them to memory. Personalize them like this: "For God so loved _____ that He gave His only begotten Son." Now put your name in that blank space. Meditate on God loving you. Concentrate upon Scriptures that build your faith and reveal God's character and heart towards you. When you feel like God is indifferent towards you, or hates you or will reject you, recite and meditate on 1 John 4:16:

> We have come to know and have believed the love which God has for us. God is love, and the one who abides in love abides in God, and God abides in him.

Embrace a life attitude of faith in the Word. Get belligerent: "Jesus commanded me to abide in His love. Therefore I believe that through His strength I will be able to abide in His love. It doesn't matter that I don't feel like I can. It doesn't matter that I'm afraid He will reject me. I choose to believe that there is access into His love for me, too! God's love is broad enough to include me, long enough to last me all of my life, high enough to overshadow me and deep enough to uphold me!" (Ephesians 3:18).

> Finally, brethren, whatever is true, whatever is honorable, whatever is right, whatever is pure, whatever is lovely, whatever is of good

repute, if there is any excellence and if anything worthy of praise, dwell on these things (Philippians 4:18).

In Scripture God is revealed as supremely glorious. He is altogether lovely. He is good. He is love. He is worthy of praise. When you are struggling with believing in His character, immerse yourself in the truth of Who He is. "Dwell on these things." As you do this, you are opening the door to faith and closing the door to unbelief. You are positioning yourself to receive revelation and the activity of the Spirit.

Now the Lord is the Spirit, and where the Spirit of the Lord is, there is liberty (2 Corinthians 3:17).

Your movement towards faith and trust in God is pleasing to Him, and remember, "He is a rewarder of those who seek Him" (Hebrews 11:6).

## Forgiveness

One key area of hindrance is unforgiveness and bitterness. Forgiveness is a critical issue. Let's start looking at this issue by taking a look at an important Biblical practice, the Year of Jubilee. Reconciliation and restoration are so important to God that He instituted the "Jubilee." The Jubilee's scope encompassed the wiping out of debts, freedom for slaves, and the restoration of land to the original owners. It is first mentioned in Leviticus:

You shall thus consecrate the fiftieth year and proclaim a release through the land to all its inhabitants. It shall be a jubilee for you, and each of you shall return to his own property, and each of you shall return to his family (Leviticus 25:10).

Israel was held responsible to keep this Jubilee year, and with obedience came a blessing. But, after centuries of rejecting this statute, judgment came:

> Therefore thus says the LORD: You have not obeyed Me in proclaim-
> ing release each man to his brother and each man to his neighbor.
> Behold, I am proclaiming a release to you – declares the LORD – to
> the sword, to the pestilence and to the famine; and I will make you
> a terror to all the kingdoms of the earth (Jeremiah 34:17).

The forgiveness of debts, restoration of lands, and freedom for
slaves were required by God if Israel wanted to maintain the blessing and favor of God. It was *legislated* forgiveness. To the extent
that they refused to forgive, to release, they would suffer the judgment of God. God took the Jubilee very seriously.

In the same way God legislated forgiveness in Israel, so Messiah
has legislated forgiveness in the Church. The Hebrew word for Jubilee is *Yovel* – it indicates "the blowing of trumpets." The sure
prophetic call to forgive others has gone out from Jesus like
the blast of a shofar. Read the entire parable found in Matthew
18:23–35. Here we will just look at a few key verses:

> Then summoning him, his lord said to him, "You wicked slave, I for-
> gave you all that debt because you pleaded with me. Should you not
> also have had mercy on your fellow slave, in the same way that I had
> mercy on you?" And his lord, moved with anger, handed him over to
> the torturers until he should repay all that was owed him. My heav-
> enly Father will also do the same to you, if each of you does not
> forgive his brother from your heart (Matthew 18:32–35).

Here is a corresponding witness:

> Therefore I say to you, all things for which you pray and ask, believe
> that you have received them, and they will be granted you. When-
> ever you stand praying, forgive, if you have anything against any-
> one, so that your Father who is in heaven will also forgive you your
> transgressions (Mark 11:24–25).

Jesus said you must forgive if you don't want to be "handed…over
to the torturers." Forgive so that you may receive forgiveness. This
is a similar principle to the Jubilee; release them, or He "releases"

you into judgment. Clearly, extending forgiveness to others is a necessity for believers who want to maintain their relationship with God and continue to grow in Him.

How does this affect the apprehension of the knowledge of the love of God? Simply put, many have difficulty experiencing the love of God because they refuse to forgive. As we discussed earlier, we must be aware that the adversary is trying to steal the word. Recognize that we've got to stir ourselves up to grasp this truth and fight to retain revelation by going to God in prayer. We can pray in faith relying upon the fact that we are loved and we will be heard. But you must also acknowledge this – if we have bitterness in our hearts we're not going to receive the grace we need. In fact, God will hand us over to the exact opposite experience of what we desire to acquire from Him. We must forgive.

This type of prayer is way too familiar:

> Yet You, O LORD, know all their deadly designs against me; do not forgive their iniquity or blot out their sin from Your sight. But may they be overthrown before You; deal with them in the time of Your anger! (Jeremiah 18:23).

God is calling us to follow a higher example:

> When they came to the place called The Skull, there they crucified Him and the criminals, one on the right and the other on the left. But Jesus was saying, "Father, forgive them; for they do not know what they are doing." And they cast lots, dividing up His garments among themselves. And the people stood by, looking on. And even the rulers were sneering at Him, saying, "He saved others; let Him save Himself if this is the Christ of God, His Chosen One." The soldiers also mocked Him, coming up to Him, offering Him sour wine, and saying, "If You are the King of the Jews, save Yourself!" (Luke 23:33–37).

When you see bitterness within your heart, bring this truth to mind: habits of resentment hinder the experience of His love. You must determine to be reconciled to all you have offended and all who have hurt you. Do you want to grasp the love of God? Answer this: is there anyone against whom you are keeping a record of wrongs? 1 Corinthians 13:5 conveys that love does not take into account a wrong *suffered*. Do you have an inability to relate to certain people without seeing them through a bitter grid? If so, pursue reconciliation.

But what does the pursuit of reconciliation look like if there is no possibility of change? There may be someone with whom, no matter how hard you try, you can never be reconciled. They deeply mistrust you; you can't trust them, etc. Reconciliation of the relationship is apparently beyond human capacity. They will never be able to "pay you back." In fact, they might not even think they owe you anything.

Remember, even if there is no forward motion in reconciliation you can still stand in a place of intercession for those who have clearly wronged you. Jesus said, "Forgive them, because they do not know what they're doing." We can be assured that this is a true diagnosis of everyone's spiritual condition, even the people who have wronged you.

Let me share another truth with you. Please read this carefully, as it can be misconstrued as an "easy way out." It's not. Ideally, the community of believers should be adequate or bring about reconciliation in every circumstance. Yet, even if the Church was mature enough, loving enough and humble enough to adjudicate most differences, not every relationship would get resolved. The truth is that there are some relational situations that are so snarled and subjective that it's just impossible to work them out. Does this mean that you are allowed to walk in bitterness? No, for God has legislated forgiveness.

The Jubilee represents and demonstrates the new birth of relationships. There will be some who are never going to be able to repay you. It is beyond their capacity to recognize that they've wronged you. I encourage you to forgive in the name of Jesus and rip up the IOUs whether they appreciate it or not. They may never acknowledge the debt or the hurt they have caused. There are some situations in which you could bring in a dozen mediators and never agree as to who owes what. Use the Jubilee principle: forgive them anyway, with a clear conscience, under the authority of the mandated law of God.

There could be people whose motivations you could never rightly trust. But you can still forgive. Remember, extending forgiveness has been legislated. We've been commanded to forgive. I am not saying to avoid the way of the cross. This also is part of the way of the cross. Forgive them and pray for them; they really don't know what they've done.

Every one of us who take reconciliation and forgiveness seriously will go through seasons of trial in our relationships. There will be times we need to be forgiven, times we need to forgive others, and times when mutual confession and forgiveness will need to be exchanged.

Good and well-meaning people may become hopelessly alienated from one another. They do not mean one another harm, yet each is thoroughly convinced of the essential righteousness of their differing perspectives.

No malice is intended. No deception employed. Yet, despite mutual respect and love, the meeting of mind and heart necessary for full reconciliation is apparently impossible. In this type of situation I encourage each to employ the Jubilee principle: Put it under the blood. Agree to disagree, do not stand against one another, but walk as friends. Seek to help one another as the opportunity arises. Agree that the unity of the Body expressed in love and peace is more important than either party being exonerated or justified.

I recognize that this is not the highest example of reconciliation, but it is much better than wanting to avoid people. This is not the highest, but it's real. You may need to do this. Remember, you don't need vindication from mere humans. If you hunger for deeper restoration, this form of forgiveness may be a first step. Bring to mind that God made a way to forgive us because He valued us. Sometimes we have to give up what is "right" in order to establish righteousness.

There may even be those who have harmed you who have died before any potential reconciliation was accomplished. You're never going to hear them say, "I'm sorry." Why not forgive? Get rid of the bitterness in your life. It's more important for you to be walking in forgiveness and freedom than it is to have everybody pay up.

After all, do you want an obligation to pay back your debt to God? Somebody already paid your debt for you. Jesus also paid for those who have offended you. Why not accept Jesus' payment of their debt before the Father as good enough for you?

Forgiveness will clear the way for you to receive. As you release others, God will likewise release you into mercy and blessing. Forgiving others (and at times, forgiving yourself) is a necessary and important key to being able to receive the love of God.

## Chapter Summary

We've been called to have a firm foundation in the love of God (Ephesians 3:17). We're called to participate in the construction of the "house" of our lives (Psalm 127:1). The Messiah encouraged us to persevere in clearing away that which is unstable and flimsy so we may rest upon the rock. Some of us have more to dig through than others (Luke 6:48). However, it is well worth the effort if the end result is having our lives founded upon the eternal dynamic love of the Trinity.

As you continue to pursue the knowledge of God's love, you might need to overcome some specific obstacles. Recognize that you have an enemy who has developed strategies against your being aware of God's love towards you. Have you cast down false teachings which are lifted up over and against the knowledge of the Lord's love? Have you made a firm decision to abide in this love, to pursue and persevere in this endeavor? Are you willing to embrace God's word of acceptance above your own feelings of rejection? Are there areas of condemnation which must be brought to His Cross as you seek to return to the Father? Is unforgiveness hindering you?

Sometimes we have to dig deep that we may rest upon something which is firm. As we engage in seeking to overcome the obstacles that are hindering us, we will find our foundation becoming more firm and sure. Though battle is involved, experiencing this love which surpasses knowledge is well worth every effort.

## Consider

To have a flourishing relationship with the Lord, we have to believe and trust His motivations towards us. Trusting His motives is necessary to understanding Him. "Good faith" must be established. Here's an illustration:

Imagine a young man, ardently in love with a young lady. He arrives at her home, carrying flowers, bringing chocolates. She opens the door. Offering tokens of affection, he says, "I love you."

"You hate me. You're just trying to make me sneeze and get me fat!" *...slam*!

Why? The motive is misconstrued. Someone's love may be real but it must be believed. The beloved may see a genuine lover as seeking to use, manipulate, control, destroy. No matter what the lover does or says, it will be mistrusted.

The painful gap between intention and perception deepens according to the degree the love is doubted. Alienation is the result of misinterpreted motives. The more important the relationship, the deeper the alienation and hurt that results from mistrust.

This is true in every relationship. It is true in your relationship with God. God loves us. To the degree we doubt His love we are going to misunderstand His activity in our lives. Do you have "good faith" towards the Lord?

1. What is the most important truth you learned in this chapter?

2. What obstacle to knowing God's love is the most difficult in your life? Can you think of a Scripture that speaks to this obstacle? Write it out and pray it through. Talk to your best friend or someone functioning in a pastoral capacity in your life about this problem.

3. Do you know of any areas of unbelief from which you must turn to further grasp God's love?

4. Other than the verses listed, can you think of another verse that speaks of forgiving others? Write out the verse and any thoughts about the verse.

5. What did you struggle with the most in this chapter? Consider taking further time to study the Scriptures about this topic, and commit it to prayer.

6. Please paraphrase, personalize and pray through 2 Corinthians 10:4–5:

   For the weapons of our warfare are not of the flesh, but divinely powerful for the destruction of fortresses. We are destroying speculations and every lofty thing raised up against the knowledge of God, and we are taking every thought captive to the obedience of Christ.

*O the deep, deep love of Jesus, love of every love the best!*
*'Tis an ocean full of blessing, 'tis a haven giving rest!*
*O the deep, deep love of Jesus, 'tis a heaven of heavens to me;*
*And it lifts me up to glory, for it lifts me up to Thee!*

SAMUEL T. FRANCIS

*I want to soak in Your love, Father, as much as it is possible.*
*In no way am I worthy. Yet You love me, You love ME! Hallelujah!*

A. W. TOZER

*It is one of the most amazing facts in all Scripture that just as God's love*
*involves his giving of himself to make us happy, so we can in return give of*
*ourselves and actually bring joy to God's heart.*

WAYNE GRUDEM, *Systematic Theology*

*I implore you in God's name, not to think of Him as hard to please, but*
*rather as generous beyond all that you can ask or think.*

ABBE DE TOURVILLE

# Chapter 12

# Pursue Love

*Therefore I say to you, all things for which you pray and ask, believe that you have received them, and they will be granted you (Mark 11:24–25).*

NOW THAT WE HAVE LOOKED at a number of hindrances, let's utilize this final chapter to discover how to overcome, how to really get hold of this love for yourself. God gives us specific directions in the Scriptures as to how to walk with Him. These instructions are very valuable to your fellowship with God. I encourage you, if you really want to grasp the love of God, to determine to walk in these ways that God has provided for us.

## Repent and Believe

We're going to begin with the first words Jesus speaks in what most believe to be the earliest Gospel, Mark:

The time is fulfilled, and the Kingdom of God is at hand; repent and believe in the good news! (Mark 1:15b).

The strengthening of your heart has to do with the building of faith. As your faith increases, there is a subsequent progressive unfolding of the realization that God loves you. God will move upon the basis of your trust and grant the revelation of His love. Jesus will open your eyes. Faith brings God into the picture. Faith moves

God. A revelation of God's love will come in response to your childlike trust. He will answer your faith-filled prayer.

> When He entered the house, the blind men came up to Him, and Jesus said to them, "Do you believe that I am able to do this?" They said to Him, "Yes, Lord." Then He touched their eyes, saying, "It shall be done to you according to your faith" (Matthew 9:28–29).

You may lament, "But my faith is so weak." Remember the father of the tormented child at the base of the Holy Mountain (2 Peter 1:18). He said, "I do believe, help my unbelief" (Mark 9:24b). He appealed to the Lord on the basis of Jesus' compassion. It's true that you can't just work faith up, but you can ask God to help your unbelief. You already believe to some extent, right? If you believe to some degree, start with that. Faith will grow if you begin to employ it.

Here's the process. You have this little bit of faith, it's like a seed. To the degree that you already believe begin to pray and act upon your faith – plant and nurture that seed. After a while you will see growth, there will be a harvest. The harvest produces more seed. If you care for the revelation it will grow. Sow the seed that has come as a result of the harvest. If you pray upon the basis of what you see by the Spirit, it will increase. Guard the seed from the adversary. Be faithful.

> Now He who supplies seed to the sower and bread for food will supply and multiply your seed for sowing and increase the harvest of your righteousness (2 Corinthians 9:10).

Pray on the basis of God's revealed will (1 John 5:14). Start with what you already believe. Mark 11:24 reveals that the Living One will answer you.

> Therefore I say to you, all things for which you pray and ask, believe that you have received them, and they will be granted you (Mark 11:24–25).

Philippians 4 instructs us to add thanksgiving to what we know God will do.

> Be anxious for nothing, but in everything by prayer and supplication with thanksgiving let your requests be made known to God (Philippians 4:6).

Act in faith. Jesus is calling you to walk on the water, trusting in His love. His mercy will cause you to know the fullness of His love. Remember the way He related to the blind man who cried, "Son of David have mercy upon me" (Luke 18:38). Did Jesus have mercy? He did. He does. He will.

Look at the way in which He related to the helpless:

> And a leper came to Him and bowed down before Him, and said, "Lord, if You are willing, You can make me clean." Jesus stretched out His hand and touched him, saying, "I am willing; be cleansed." And immediately his leprosy was cleansed" (Matthew 8:2–3).

Pray: "Lord, if You are willing, You can destroy the false concepts of the way I view you. You can heal me of error's effects upon my life. Lord, if You are willing, You can cleanse me."

Jesus had mercy on the blind man. He healed the leper. What do you think Jesus' response to your prayer will be?

I want to note one other thing. Some people's faith might be hindered by a fear of getting out of His will, of losing a passion for ministry, of somehow getting sidetracked or stopped in their tracks. Yet, isn't it true that the Scriptures teach that Jesus loves you? Isn't it true that we are commanded to abide in His love? When it comes to Jesus loving you, what are you called to believe that's false? The Scripture clearly reveals His love for us. Jesus and the Apostles incorporated God's love into their lives in a personal, deep, and ongoing way. Doesn't He want us to follow His example in knowing that Father loves us? Did He command us to abide in His love to cause us to become unfruitful? If we know that God truly does love us and we apply that truth to our lives, we do not need to fear being deceived. He is good! He will use your pursuit of knowing His love for your good and the benefit of those around you. Trust Him.

## Make an Effort – Pursue His Love

Another practical step we can take is to make a determination to put some effort into pursuing this love. Now, it is true that spiritual progress is not dependent upon human effort. No matter how hard you strive you can't achieve growth. Paul wrote, "It is God Who gives the increase" (1 Corinthians 3:7). Paradoxically, there is usually no spiritual growth without human co-labor.

> Unless the LORD builds the house, they labor in vain who build it; unless the LORD guards the city, the watchman keeps awake in vain (Psalm 127:1).

This verse tells us that God builds, yet the workers still labor. There is work involved. The point is, we can labor on our own, or in cooperation with God. When God is involved, then it is fruitful labor. Spiritual growth comes from blessed effort – God's working with us to produce the increase. God has revealed that He is willing to co-labor with us to help produce true spiritual growth. Apart from Him we can do nothing, but with Him spiritual growth can transpire.

Building upon the foundation of faith in God, we should make a faith-filled dependent effort towards apprehending this love. We must make a decision to enter into this labor. Do you want to apprehend God's love? Decide to do so. Decide to pursue. Decide to expend effort towards this end. Choose to labor with God to build this knowledge in your life. He will help you. He wants you to know His love (John 15:9).

Once this decision is made, it is wise to consecrate yourself to the Lord in this area. Something along the lines of: "Father, I believe you want me to know Your love. I believe Your love is for me. I want to know this love. I commit myself to You for the purpose of pursuing this love."

**Draw me after you and let us run together! (Song of Solomon 1:4a).**

Inseparable from this commitment is asking His help to persevere and obtain. As we noted, the worker labors in vain unless God builds the house. Therefore *ask* God to "build the house." Pray along these lines: "Lord, I recognize that left to my own devices I will never grasp Your love. I believe that the knowledge of Your love comes from You through the help of the Holy Spirit. Please anoint me to grasp the love of God. Please help me make a real effort to pursue this goal."

These are simple steps, but they can help you build a solid foundation from which to "pursue."

## Abiding in Jesus

Another aspect of pursuing has to do with simply maintaining your relationship with God.

Working together with the principle of God building the house, we find that spiritual growth comes from consistently abiding in Jesus' love. Here's the process: we faithfully maintain our relationship with God. We take time to meet with Him. We take time for prayer, to study the Scriptures, to meditate on the Word. We invest ourselves in godly and committed fellowship with other believers. Growth comes as we respond to God by the power He gives.

As we abide in Jesus through maintaining our relationship with Him, He moves in our lives. After all, in John 15, abiding is the key to the life of Jesus flowing through you. "Apart from Me you can do nothing" (John 15:5). Remember the prayer from Ephesians 3. It is written that through Jesus abiding in our Spirit-strengthened souls, we will be enabled to grasp His love. Staying in this close fellowship with Jesus is the means and the goal of our spiritual lives. As we abide in Him, we are transformed by His activity. We are strengthened by His Spirit. We begin to grasp His love. Our part of this equation is drawing near to God.

Read James 4:8a: "Draw near to God and He will draw near to you." As you draw near, He will respond, and His activity will transform your relationship with Him.

## Prayer

Prayer provides God with the "legal right" to invade the "god of this world's" territory (2 Corinthians 4:4).

> The whole world lies in the power of the evil one (1 John 5:19b).

> Your kingdom come, Your will be done, on earth as it is in heaven (Matthew 6:10).

The Lord has determined that we must ask Him into situations. Here's an analogy: in the same way we must ask Jesus to save us, though He is already a Savior, so we must ask God to exercise sovereignty though He is the rightful King and has all power.

> And He said to them, "It is written, 'My house shall be called a house of prayer' " (Matthew 21:13).

We are God's "house of prayer" in the earth (enemy territory). You know that you are loved by God. Pray to God about apprehending His love in reliance upon this foundational truth.

John 16:25 states, "I will tell you plainly about My Father." Please read the immediate context of this statement:

> These things I have spoken to you in figurative language; an hour is coming when I will no longer speak to you in figurative language, but will tell you plainly of the Father. In that day you will ask in My name,

and I do not say to you that I will request of the Father on your behalf; for the Father Himself loves you, because you have loved Me and have believed that I came forth from the Father (John 16:25–27).

What is it Jesus wants to tell us *plainly of the Father?* I believe one thing He wants to tell us is that "the Father Himself loves you because you have loved (Jesus) and have believed that (He) came forth from the Father" (John 16:27). Jesus, knowing His Father's heart, communicated the Father's heart. He determined to reveal Father's *agape* to these men. This heart has not changed. It is the will of God that you should know His love. Therefore, pray in faith for yourself and others. We are invited to place our faith in God through asking Him into every situation in our lives. Exercise your faith and begin to pray!

Let's follow Paul's example in Ephesians 3 and join him in supplication – begging – for God to reveal His love to you.

The prayer of a righteous man is powerful and effective (James 5:16).

This is the confidence which we have before Him, that, if we ask anything according to His will, He hears us. And if we know that He hears us in whatever we ask, we know that we have the requests which we have asked from Him (1 John 5:14–15).

Then you will call upon Me and come and pray to Me, and I will listen to you. You will seek Me and find Me when you search for Me with all your heart (Jeremiah 29:12–13).

If seeking God is important, why not make it a priority? God wants you to know the truth about Him. He wants you to know Him as He knows Himself (that's why He has given you His Spirit). According to John and Paul, that is our destiny! (1 John 3:2; 1 Corinthians 13:12). God knows Himself as the God Who is love. We see this blessed relationship within the Trinity. He's put His Spirit within us so that by His Spirit we're crying out, "Abba." He is the same Spirit that Jesus has.

Let's apply ourselves to seeking God. Not only is this an appropriate and obedient response, but there are so many benefits that proceed from knowing the love of God, and they can be yours. If you want those benefits, then cry out to God for a revelation. Pledge your heart to intercede for yourself, your congregation, Jesus' body; ask for the knowledge of the love of the Messiah.

At times spiritual growth requires discipline and even aggression. If you want to grow in the Spirit, if you want to remove barriers to knowing the love of God and deal with the resistance you may find in your own heart, then you must take the offensive, be warlike. Sometimes we need to employ prayer and travail with fasting to prevail. If you are struggling to break through, consider applying more discipline in pursuing a breakthrough. Consider fasting and ask: "Abba, if this is indeed as important as I believe it is, please reveal it to me. Change my life."

A helpful way to approach praying for the love of God is praying through Scripture. We have encouraged you to pray through Ephesians 3:14–21. I once assigned a class to pray through that passage daily for more than a month! That might seem monotonous; however, the testimony of the students was that they were receiving revelation, being strengthened, and increasing in faith through this exercise. It was a help to them.

If you are praying through a petition penned by a holy Apostle then you are praying in God's will and can confidently believe the Lord wants this prayer answered. In addition, oftentimes as we pray through the Word, we are "meditating" upon it, and it gets more deeply into our hearts and minds. This can lead to revelation.

This prayer, to know the breadth, length, height and depth of the love of the Messiah Jesus, can provide a platform of confidence, can help open the door to revelation, and can help you more deeply receive the Word of God. I encourage you to pray through Scriptures concerning the love of God. Pray through Galatians 2:20b. Pray through John 15:9. Pray through John 3:16. The prayer in Ephesians 3 is especially relevant to the pursuit of God's love. Pray through Ephesians 3:14–21. This will help you.

> For this reason I bow my knees before the Father, from whom every family in heaven and on earth derives its name, that He would grant you, according to the riches of His glory, to be strengthened with power through His Spirit in the inner man, so that Christ may dwell in your hearts through faith; and that you, being rooted and grounded in love, may be able to comprehend with all the saints what is the breadth and length and height and depth, and to know the love of Christ which surpasses knowledge, that you may be filled up to all the fullness of God (Ephesians 3:14–19).

After this petition Paul gives this doxology:

> Now to Him who is able to do far more abundantly beyond all that we ask or think, according to the power that works within us, to Him be the glory in the church and in Christ Jesus to all generations forever and ever. Amen (Ephesians 3:20–21).

It is possible to be filled "up to all the fullness of God" because there is a God Who is able to bring this to pass. Why not use this prayer, not as some sort of stale ritual but as a format and a foundation for crying out.

"God, do this in me! Strengthen me in my innermost being. Let Jesus dwell in my heart through faith, conveying and interpreting the love of God to my soul. Lord, I want to be growing into, rooted in, grounded in, and founded upon this love. I want to grasp it for myself. I want to have this type of stability. Reveal it to me. Let me have this by the Spirit. I want to know **You**."

Paul was not petitioning God for an intellectual conviction. The Apostle was asking for the conversion of hearts and a sacred intuitive knowledge. I am not opposed, obviously, to having a Biblical and doctrinal understanding of the love of God. "To the law and to the testimony! If they do not speak according to this word, it is because they have no dawn" (Isaiah 8:20). In this life, the Word of God is the supreme arbiter and evaluator of spiritual truth. Through it we can have a foundational knowledge that God really loves us and that Jesus is saying, "Abide in My love."

Still, the Apostle Paul was praying for these people by the Spirit. Let's submit to the grace upon Paul's life, jump into that anointing and call upon the Lord for revelation. We can be convinced through "revelation."

There is a revelatory walk and relationship that we are to have with Him. According to John 17:3, eternal life is the knowledge of God. He Who revealed Messiah to you will reveal His love to you as well. Don't doubt. He will, for it is His will.

## Study and Meditation

Something else you can do to grow and remove barriers is: apply yourself to study and meditation. Receiving truth is similar to receiving a present. The recipient anticipates, unwraps, admires, thanks, reads the instructions, uses and enjoys the gift. This is the way we should "receive" the Word. Apply this process to the Scriptures. You have to concentrate upon the Scriptures and apply the Word by faith to your need to know God's love. Then do it again. Study.

Meditation is a helpful practice which can aid us in successfully abiding in the love of God. There are several Hebrew words which are translated "meditate" in the Old Testament. These words contain the idea of speaking something over and over, really considering a matter, pondering, muttering or musing.

Meditation is similar to working through concepts and memorizing facts when you face an important exam. It is looking to God for

truth in the Scriptures in the same way you would search for a
street sign so you might get to an important appointment in an
unfamiliar city.

Everyone meditates. Practically everyone has meditated in the Biblical fashion, but not necessarily on the truths of the Word. When-
ever you've seen someone so aggravated that they're talking to themselves, you've seen meditation. If you've ever muttered to yourself
because of anxiety, that's meditation. It is meditation, but it's ori-
ented in the wrong direction.

Ultimately, Biblical meditation is being engaged and engrossed in
the truths of Scripture to the degree that you just can't help thinking or talking about them. When you pray through a Bible passage,
and think about what you're praying, you're meditating. When you
are putting a melody to Scripture and concentrating on what you
sing, you're meditating. When you are spending time studying some
verses, thinking about their meanings, you're meditating. If you are
considering the intent of a passage you're memorizing, you're involved in meditation. If you receive some illumination by the Holy
Spirit on a Biblical passage and hold on to it, and consider it in
God's presence – you're meditating.

Another key to meditation is remembering. Remembrance is part
of Biblical tradition. There is something wonderful about having a
sacred calendar. Within the framework of the Jewish sacred calendar are days like Purim and Chanukah. Purim is the Feast of Esther.
Was that commemoration commanded by the Lord? No. Its origin
was similar to this, "God did this incredible thing for us, let's remember it every single year!" The same is true with Chanukah, the
Feast of Dedication. We know Jesus celebrated that holiday:

> At that time the Feast of the Dedication took place at Jerusalem; it
> was winter, and Jesus was walking in the temple in the portico of
> Solomon (John 10:22–23).

As part of your personal tradition of remembrance, I encourage you to journal. As part of your meditation, as a means to remember, take time and write the things you believe God is revealing to you about Himself. I've had experiences with God which are very important to me. I mark the anniversaries of these events by recording the dates in my journals in advance. They are my own private holy days. I commemorate these events because I want to remember them in His presence. For instance, I remember the day I gave my life to Jesus and started walking as a disciple. I remember the hour. I remember who was talking with me. I remember.

Study the Word. Meditate upon the Word of God. Remember your own history with God. Record the things that the Lord has done and review them with thanksgiving.

## Sowing and Reaping

Sowing and reaping is a primary spiritual principle. It can be employed as a means to knowing the love of God.

> Do not be deceived, God is not mocked; for whatever a man sows, this he will also reap. For the one who sows to his own flesh will from the flesh reap corruption, but the one who sows to the Spirit will from the Spirit reap eternal life (Galatians 6:7–8).

In Hosea 10:12 we are exhorted to:

> Sow with a view to righteousness, reap in accordance with kindness; break up your fallow ground, for it is time to seek the LORD until He comes to rain righteousness on you.

Using this principle, we can sow with a view towards receiving the knowledge of God's love. Everything we've discussed thus far has been individualistic, almost inward. Sowing gives you another tool: action. You can rely upon the God Who has ordained the law of sowing and reaping and begin to act in faith.

God has determined cycles since the dawn of time. Sowing and reaping is the first and foundational type of a vital cycle. Read this:

> While the earth remains, seedtime and harvest, and cold and heat, and summer and winter, and day and night shall not cease (Genesis 8:22).

Just as, in agriculture, one can sow and reap a harvest, so also, in spiritual things, we are able to deliberately sow. How? Through acting in faith.

Look at this principle: "And anything not based on faith is sin" (Romans 14:23b). Although this is a word of warning, it is not a word of bondage. What does this mean in relation to the love of God? How does it relate to sowing and reaping?

Look at these two verses:

> How blessed is the one whom You choose and bring near to You to dwell in Your courts (Psalm 65:4a).

> Draw near to God and He will draw near to you (James 4:8a).

It is right to hope in God's initiation and in His response to our holy action. Have confidence that there is a God and He causes things to happen. Believe we will stand before Him in the judgment and be evaluated for all we have done. We're going to have to give an account for our actions. We're going to reap what we've sown in this life. This is not necessarily a negative thing.

> For I am conscious of nothing against myself, yet I am not by this acquitted; but the one who examines me is the Lord. Therefore do not go on passing judgment before the time, but wait until the Lord comes who will both bring to light the things hidden in the darkness and disclose the motives of men's hearts; and then each man's praise will come to him from God (1 Corinthians 4:4–5).

If you have this assurance, act. Take action, believing there is a God Who sees and will cause you to reap the consequences of what you do. That's the beginning of wisdom. It's called *the fear of the Lord.*

> Therefore we also have as our ambition, whether at home or absent, to be pleasing to Him. For we must all appear before the judgment seat of Christ, so that each one may be recompensed for his deeds in the body, according to what he has done, whether good or bad. Therefore, knowing the fear of the Lord, we persuade men (2 Corinthians 5:9–11a).

God has determined to uphold this law of sowing and reaping. He established this law and He honors what He established. This is not just an absolute truth concerning final judgment, but this principle is generally true, now.

Sowing and reaping does not have to be a threatening thought. Contained in this principle is an opportunity. The purpose of sowing is to reap according to what one sows. Receiving the reality of this principle is like getting an angelic visitation in 1970 and having an angel say, "There is going to come a day when thou shalt hear of a man named Bill Gates. And this person is going to start a firm and it's going to go public and be called Microsoft. Thou art to sell everything that thou dost own and buy into that." Someone with such a revelation would be overjoyed at the opportunity to sow into Microsoft. Do not allow the truth about sowing and reaping to become a word of bondage. Begin to sow with faith. Sow wisely. Seize today's opportunities.

Sowing and reaping is a common theme of wisdom literature, like the Proverbs. Yet, the Lord Jesus, Himself, put His seal on this elementary wisdom in Luke 6:38:

> Give, and it will be given to you. They will pour into your lap a good measure – pressed down, shaken together, and running over. For by your standard of measure it will be measured to you in return.

We are functioning in faith when we believe we will reap what we sow. The Apostle Paul rehearsed these principles to the churches he discipled:

> Do not be deceived, God is not mocked; for whatever a man sows, this he will also reap. For the one who sows to his own flesh will from the flesh reap corruption, but the one who sows to the Spirit will from the Spirit reap eternal life. Let us not lose heart in doing good, for in due time we will reap if we do not grow weary. So then, while we have opportunity, let us do good to all people, and especially to those who are of the household of the faith (Galatians 6:7–10).

> With good will render service, as to the Lord, and not to men, knowing that whatever good thing each one does, this he will receive back from the Lord, whether slave or free (Ephesians 6:7–8).

Do you believe you will reap what you sow? We act in faith when we realize that every action and attitude is seed which will ultimately yield an abundant harvest (Romans 14:23b). Do you want Messiah to reveal His love to you? Demonstrate love to others unto the Lord.

What type of love do you want to know?

*Revealed, dynamic, sacrificial love!*

What type of love is it you should sow?

*Manifested, sacrificial, devoted love!*

Sow *agape*. Sow love in faith. Sow love with an expectation of receiving the same from: "God Who causes the growth" (1 Corinthians 3:7b). We serve God, Who gives the increase.

When you start to deliberately sow love, your perspective of the world changes. Suddenly everybody around you becomes an opportunity to sow the love of God *so that* you may receive back the same from the Lord. Admittedly, this is a difficult perspective to maintain, but the law of sowing and reaping is worthy of meditation…and it's Biblical.

Employing this principle combines passionate desire, the fear of the Lord and walking in wisdom. I find this path to be beautiful. This is a way to act lovingly and responsibly towards others because you want to love God and know His love. It is loving others because you love and desire God. We do the highest good for others when we serve God.

Do you want to know what it is like to be viewed as valuable by God? View others as valuable. Treat them that way in faith. The believer is especially beloved by God. Yet, it is also true that God *loves* the world. He *loves* Israel and the nations. He *loves* the lost. He loves each and every one of them (and you) with the *agape* which we have discovered in this study. Let Him communicate His heart for the world to your heart. Seek to see others as He sees them.

I encourage you to enter into God's perspective of lost humanity. Consider His heart; consider His desire to reclaim them. Do you want to experience the LORD being involved in your interests? Embrace Messiah's purposes for unredeemed humanity as your own. Do you desire to know the power of this *agape* that sent His Son to Calvary? Be involved with this aspect of His concerns. Enter into your part of the Commission Jesus gave to the witnesses of His Resurrection.

> All authority has been given to Me in heaven and on earth. Go therefore and make disciples of all the nations, baptizing them in the name of the Father and the Son and the Holy Spirit, teaching them to observe all that I commanded you; and lo, I am with you always, even to the end of the age (Matthew 28:18b–20).

Another aspect of viewing others as God views them involves treasuring the people around you. Do you wish to receive communication from the Lord? Please answer this: who needs to receive communication from you? Is it a parent? Is it a spouse? Is it a child? Is it a friend? Is it someone who is way down your social totem pole? Do you want God to pay attention to you? Have relationships with those who are "lowly." Do these things unto the Lord. You won't be disappointed.

> Do not be haughty in mind, but associate with the lowly (Romans 12:16b).

Do you wish to have a better hold on what the Spirit has been teaching you through this book? Sow the truths you have learned in other believers. Seek to bring those who don't know God into contact with the God Who loves them. As you make what you have really come to know real to others, the desire you have for the reality of God's love will become more solid. As you reveal this love to others, it will also be revealed to you.

In obedience to God's leading, with an eye towards receiving the same from the Lord, look for ways to sacrificially give yourself to the Lord. Minister to others. Spend time in praise, worship, fasting and prayer for His purposes. Give money to the Lord's work and to those in need. Love and serve your household, Jesus' Body, the lost, the needy, Israel, your own nation, other nations. Deliberately sow. In fact, *sow yourself*. See yourself as a seed, give yourself to God and allow the Lord to sow you!

> And He said, "The one who sows the good seed is the Son of Man, and the field is the world; and as for the good seed, these are the sons of the kingdom; and the tares are the sons of the evil one" (Matthew 13:37–38).

This might cost you aspects of your life to which you are clinging. Remember this principle:

> Truly, truly, I say to you, unless a grain of wheat falls into the earth and dies, it remains alone; but if it dies, it bears much fruit. He who loves his life loses it, and he who hates his life in this world will keep it to life eternal (John 12:24–25).

Ultimately, the sown seed "bears much fruit." As you allow yourself to be sown in prayer, in teaching, in loving, in forgiving, in reaching out, in giving yourself away, you will bear fruit; the harvest is worth the cost of sowing. Remember, "whatever a man sows, this he will also reap" (Galatians 6:7b). It's a promise.

## Closing

We've covered an extensive amount of material in this chapter. We've looked at primary ways to pursue knowing the love of God. Through prayer, determination, faith in the Word, meditation, forgiveness of others, and sowing and reaping, you will be enabled to progress in your knowledge of the love of God. These things are done upon the foundation of faith in the Gospel. The knowledge of the love of God is a gift. It's a gift which has a purpose – the satisfying of hearts, God's heart and ours.

As I close this chapter of practical instruction, I encourage you to be delivered from any form of frantic action. These means of following after God are not to be done out of soulish desperation, but out of a determined faith-filled pursuit. Our attitude must be, "This is something I want to cultivate. This is something I must have. This is something God desires for me. This is something I am going to work at. This is something God is going to do. I will work and I will trust the Lord."

May your heart be encouraged in this pursuit through the truth that God loves you and has made a way for you to come near. He wants you to know His love and has given you His Spirit as a Helper. He is initiating; you are responding. In His love, He will make a way; His love is available to you right now. You have been created and redeemed towards this end: to know this love that surpasses knowledge, to be filled with the fullness of God.

We're going to close with Romans 8:31–39. I encourage you to read it aloud and spend time meditating upon it.

> What then shall we say to these things? If God is for us, who is against us? He who did not spare His own Son, but delivered Him over for us all, how will He not also with Him freely give us all things? Who will bring a charge against God's elect? God is the one who justifies; who is the one who condemns? Christ Jesus is He who died, yes, rather who was raised, who is at the right hand of God, who also intercedes for us. Who will separate us from the love of Christ? Will tribulation, or distress, or persecution, or famine, or nakedness, or peril, or sword? Just as it is written, "For Your sake we are being put to death all day long, we were considered as sheep to be slaughtered." But in all these things we overwhelmingly conquer through Him who loved us. For I am convinced that neither death, nor life, nor angels, nor principalities, nor things present, nor things to come, nor powers, nor height, nor depth, nor any other created thing, will be able to separate us from the love of God, which is in Christ Jesus our Lord (Romans 8:31–39).

## Consider

One path to grasping is through personal encounters with God. Along with the Scripture, the Father often gives experiences that become touchstones in life. Ask God for experiences with Him that will help you to abide by faith in His love for you. In response to prayer, the "Father of glory" is able to "give to you a spirit of wisdom and of revelation in the knowledge of Him" (Ephesians 1:17b).

God instructed Jeremiah, "Call to Me and I will answer you, and I will tell you great and mighty [guarded] things, which you do not know" (Jeremiah 33:3).

Through the Spirit, God can grant you revelation about Himself and His love which will be life changing. Ask for the Spirit of Revelation. Pray like this: "Lord, I do not yet know this love as I ought.

I'm feeling like I'm getting some sort of a grip on it, but please reveal more. I'm not asking for an experience apart from your Word; give me illumination by Your Word. Show me by the Spirit. Reveal Yourself to me." Perhaps God will choose a day and pour His love upon you in a way that you will remember for the rest of your life.

1. What is the most important truth you learned in this chapter?

2. List three Scriptures mentioned in this chapter that contain principles that may help you to grasp the love of Jesus. What are those principles?

3. Are you aware of any cycles in your life? If so, do you know why? Write out your answers and pray about it.

4. Name three ways you can sow seeds of love in a friend's life to reap a revelation of God's love for you.

5. As a result of reading and working through this book, do you feel competent to teach these foundational principles to others? How would you use the Scriptures to counsel someone who has despaired of ever knowing God's love?

6. What did you struggle with the most in this chapter? Consider taking further time to study the Scriptures about this topic, and commit it to prayer.

7. Please paraphrase, personalize and pray through John 16:27:

    For the Father Himself loves you, because you have loved Me and have believed that I came forth from the Father.

# Bibliography

Ferguson, Sinclair B., David F. Wright, and J.I. Packer *eds. New Dictionary of Theology,* Downers Grove, IL: InterVarsity Press, 1988.

Fox, Matthew. Breakthrough: Meister Eckhardt's Creation Spirituality in *New Translation, Introduction and Commentarie,* Garden City, NY: Image Books, Doubleday & Company, Inc., 1980.

Louw, Johannes P., and Eugene A. Nida. *Greek-English Lexicon of the New Testament based on Semantic Domains,* 2nd Edition, New York, NY: United Bible Societies, 1988.

Lucado, Max. *Experiencing the Heart of Jesus,* Nashville, TN: Thomas Nelson, 2003.

Morris, Leon. *Testaments of Love: A Study of Love in the Bible,* Downer's Grove, IL: William B. Eerdmans Publishing Co., 1981.

Nygren, Anders and Philip S. Watson *translator. Agape and Eros,* Philadelphia, PA: Westminster Press, 1953.

Packer, J.I. *Knowing God,* Downers Grove, IL: InterVarsity Press, 1993.

Thayer, Joseph. *Thayer's Greek-English Lexicon of the New Testament,* Peabody, MA: Hendrickson Publishers, 1996.

*The New Spirit Filled Life Bible,* Nashville, TN: Thomas Nelson, 2002.

# About the *Love of God* Project

THE *LOVE OF GOD* PROJECT is a long term undertaking by a team of believers joined together in a single purpose: educating the body of Messiah about the love of God. Our desire is for every believer to come to deeply and personally know the love of the Messiah, and to be enabled to effectively pass it on to the world. We believe that we have received a mandate to help serve this purpose. To this end, we are developing materials which will teach, train, inspire, challenge, edify, and aid individual believers from every stratum of life and in every aspect of ministry.

To date, the *Love of God* Project has developed:

| | |
|---|---|
| A 4-hour seminar for adults | This book |
| A children's worship CD | A coloring book |
| An adults' worship CD | Supplemental study materials |
| Teaching Series (available on CD) | |

As we continue to seek to be faithful to this mandate we will be working on translating materials into other languages, creating additional devotional and in-depth study materials, and training others who have a heart to know and spread the good news of God's love.

As the Project has developed, the Lord has continued to link us with individuals who have similar hearts. We welcome others who have experienced the love of God and want to help in releasing it to join with us in developing materials. We welcome those with intercessory calls to pray for the ongoing development of the project. We welcome those with financial and material resources who would like to sow into this project. We also welcome those with questions and those who desire further interaction about the love of God.

Here's our website: www.LoveofGodproject.org
Feel free to write us at: LoveofGodproject@gmail.com

We're glad you worked through the book and look forward to hearing from you.